Chauncey
Yellow Robe

Chauncey Yellow Robe

A Biography of the American Indian Educator, ca. 1870–1930

DAVID W. MESSER

Foreword by RONA YELLOW ROBE

McFarland & Company, Inc., Publishers
Jefferson, North Carolina

LIBRARY OF CONGRESS CATALOGUING-IN-PUBLICATION DATA

Names: Messer, David W., 1948– author.
Title: Chauncey Yellow Robe : a biography of the American Indian educator, ca. 1870–1930 / David W. Messer ; foreword by Rona Yellow Robe.
Description: Jefferson, North Carolina : McFarland & Company, Inc., 2018 | Includes bibliographical references and index.
Identifiers: LCCN 2018041755 | ISBN 9781476673226 (softcover : acid free paper) ♾
Subjects: LCSH: Yellow Robe, Chauncey, 1870–1930. | Lakota Indians—Biography. | Indian educators—Biography. | LCGFT: Biographies.
Classification: LCC E99.T34 M47 2018 | DDC 370.92 [B] —dc23
LC record available at https://lccn.loc.gov/2018041755

BRITISH LIBRARY CATALOGUING DATA ARE AVAILABLE

ISBN (print) 978-1-4766-7322-6
ISBN (ebook) 978-1-4766-3304-6

© 2018 David W. Messer. All rights reserved

No part of this book may be reproduced or transmitted in any form or by any means, electronic or mechanical, including photocopying or recording, or by any information storage and retrieval system, without permission in writing from the publisher.

Front cover image of Chauncey Yellow Robe, Rapid City, South Dakota, on May 22, 1906 (courtesy of Minnilusa Historical Association, Rapid City)

Printed in the United States of America

McFarland & Company, Inc., Publishers
  Box 611, Jefferson, North Carolina 28640
  www.mcfarlandpub.com

Table of Contents

Foreword by Rona Yellow Robe   1
Preface   5
Introduction   9
"Chauncey Yellow Robe" by Badger Clark   11

1. Lakota Creation Story   13
2. Pratt Comes Calling   16
3. Canowicakte's Early Life   20
4. Clothes, Hair and Names   24
5. Killing the Indian   33
6. Chauncey in the White City   42
7. Thriving in an Unlikely Environment   48
8. A Demented Indian   50
9. The Indian Service School System   54
10. On the Move   60
11. The Rapid City Indian School   65
12. Lillian   73
13. Relationship to Sitting Bull   77
14. The Society of American Indians   81
15. Carlos Montezuma   86

Table of Contents

16.	World War I	91
17.	The Spanish Flu	101
18.	Wounded Knee and Wild West Shows	108
19.	*The Silent Enemy*	115
20.	Latter Years	129
21.	The Yellow Robe Daughters	133
22.	Chauncey's Death	141
23.	Yellow Robes	145
24.	The Yellow Robe Name	151

Chapter Notes	155
Bibliography	167
Index	171

Foreword
by Rona Yellow Robe

My name is Rona Yellow Robe. A Cree woman with African American blood, adopted by my father, Joseph Yellow Robe, who is Assinaboine and Gros Ventre from Fort Peck, Montana. However, my dad was born and raised in Havre, Montana, and resides there still. Due to the politics of enrollment in Fort Peck, my brothers and sisters and I are enrolled members of the Chippewa-Cree Tribe of Rocky Boy, Montana, under the bloodline of our mother. Our mother was Lucille Chapican-Yellow Robe, who was of the Cree Nation. She was a full-blooded Cree from Saskatchewan, Canada, who was enrolled at and lived much of her childhood on the Piapot Reserve. Because of treaties, my mother, along with many of our Canadian family, was allowed to be enrolled in both the States and Canada. Our mother passed away in January 2005. She was 63 years old.

Two years ago, I was asked to participate in Canada's Truth and Reconciliation Commission, which sheds light on the Indian mission schools and brings healing to its survivors. As children, these survivors were taken by law from their homes and forced to be educated and raised by those who did not have a clue about how to raise aboriginal children. Our mother was one of these children.

A few years before my mom passed, she and I took a road trip to her Piapot Reserve. She showed me the humble means of her childhood home, and filled me with the stories of her time there. We traveled to the Lebret mission school in Fort Qu'Appelle where she was sent to be "educated." She told of how she was taught to speak French and English. She went on to share how she and my aunties and her cousins would run away from the school only to be caught and then severely punished. Mom told me about the humiliation of getting her hair chopped off, and how she was

Foreword by Rona Yellow Robe

not allowed to speak Cree. If she did, she endured punishment as a result. As I am my mother's daughter, I can attest to being affected by her experiences long before I knew the words "intergenerational trauma."

I was flattered to be asked to write the foreword. But then, the deeper I read this book, the more I began to feel resistance to writing this piece. I sat in the comfort of my home, overlooking the beauty of the swaying trees and drinking my cup of coffee, a woman educated through the American school system, and it seemed to me that it may be easy to judge Chauncey as a sellout, an "apple." "Apple" is cruel word I heard as a young girl, used to describe an Indian who was red on the outside and white on the inside. We may think we would have been more like Montezuma, who appeared to stand strong for the culture of the indigenous people. However, as my father said, "It is important to introduce the state of the nation Chauncey lived in, and having not lived in that time, choices were much more stark." David W. Messer does well in addressing the state of the nation.

According to David's research, it is important to consider that Chauncey was a child of the Lakota people. His life was celebrated in the ceremonial ways of the Lakota Sioux. As a young boy, against his wishes, he was made to go to Carlisle Indian Institute. He was received favorably under the eye of the founder of the school, General Pratt. Like all young boys who desire a father-son relationship, a father to look up to, General Pratt became that father figure to Chauncey.

Chauncey was considered a success according to the idea of "Kill the Indian but not the man." Nevertheless, it looks to me that Chauncey survived his experience of assimilation. A child learns and picks up what is happening around him. To communicate, a child learns to speak the language. To receive love and affection, a child obeys.

Though Chauncey became an advocate for assimilating the Indian into "civilization," I could see from this biography where he used his prestige in his later years for the betterment of his people and to protect the Indian culture and traditions. Some people may not be able to see Chauncey's goodness. It is one thing to be betrayed by a government, but when it appears that one is attempting to kill the sovereignty of one's own people, it is a crime beyond treason. However, I don't believe that's what happened with Chauncey Yellow Robe. I do see a spirit who took a tough situation and made it work for him and his family.

The older I become, the more I no longer live in the limited and strict

Foreword by Rona Yellow Robe

world of right or wrong, good or bad, black or white. The famous quote "Don't judge a man until you walked two moons in his moccasins" is necessary for us to consider as we read this biography of Chauncey Yellow Robe. I'm sure, in Chauncey's own reflection upon his life, like many of us, he considered what he might have done differently. I do believe he did the best he could. Maya Angelou wisely said, "Do the best you can until you know better. Then when you know better, do better." This was demonstrated by Chauncey.

I experienced many emotions as I read about Chauncey's life. I self-righteously judged, and as I read further and was given direction from my father and best friend to look beyond my own experience in life, I compassionately forgave. Tears filled my eyes and then I would find myself laughing out loud.

David's biography is an informative and intriguing read. I am very appreciative of the research and historical information that I did not know. For example, I knew the history of Wounded Knee, but I never knew the details of the first gunfire. My father wisely told me: "Rona, you don't have to agree with everything, but it's important to understand the distance Chauncey came from those conditions. The fact that the American Indian has survived is a testament to the strength we've had to endure to make it."

I am Rona Yellow Robe. A Cree woman with African American blood, adopted Assinaboine Sioux and Gros Ventre. I do not speak my mother's or my father's language, and I only know one Cree song, which I hold very close. I have taught myself how to jingle dress dance. I've taught myself how to play the Native American flute, both traditional and contemporary style. I've never lived on my reservation in Rocky Boy, Montana, and I am educated in the schools of white America.

Some would look at my life say that I am a successful "urban Indian" woman. If those who worked to assimilate the indigenous people into the culture of white America were to look at my life, they would probably feel they succeeded. However, right at the surface of my being there is a longing, a yearning to receive back that which was taken from me long before I was born. It makes me wonder if Chauncey Yellow Robe felt the same way.

Rona Yellow Robe is a singer-songwriter and Native American Music Award–winning Flute Player of the Year for 2014 and 2016.

Preface

Chauncey Yellow Robe generally is not considered to be an iconic figure in either the real or imagined history of Native Americans. However, his story is unique and compelling. After leaving Rosebud Sioux Reservation as a young man he went to the Carlisle Indian School and then on to a measure of success that few of his Native contemporaries ever achieved. Chauncey's adult life straddled the red and white worlds. His complicated story requires considering historical and contemporary contexts, so I have attempted to tell the story of his life chronologically and thematically.

When I first started research for this book, one of Chauncey Yellow Robe's relatives told me, "White people sure think that they know Indian history more than the Indians themselves. I get the impression that you only believe what's in writing." All that I had thought I had done was to ask a couple of questions. However, I quickly learned that being white and trying to write a biography of a Native American could create problems for some people.

I am subject to the criticism that I cannot, in any way, relate to the Native way of feeling, thinking, or seeing. Neither I nor my family is experiencing the historical or intergenerational trauma that is so much a part of the Native American story and especially reservation life. I can only repeat boarding school experiences endured by others. I have not dealt with broken treaties, genocidal military and political campaigns, relocation, or any number of other atrocities—past or present. These claims are obviously correct. In many or most ways I cannot truly relate, but Chauncey Yellow Robe's life and story need to be told, and I can tell it. There are bits and pieces about him in numerous places, but there is not a complete accounting. I have approached this project objectively and have called on many Native Americans for their input, perceptions and

Preface

opinions. They have been quick to let me know where and when I might be off base and what parts of my narrative might be problematic for an Indian audience.

In 1871, A.B. Meacham, the superintendent of Indian Affairs of Oregon speaking at a Council at the Umatilla Indian reservation, correctly predicted that Indian children "will only know the history of their fathers by tradition and the history of the White Man's books."[1] Unfortunately, they have lost too much of that history just that way, and this is yet another one of those "white man" books that only partially tells the story. However, there are many positive signs that Native historians and traditionalists are reasserting possession of their story. I hope that my account of the life of Chauncey Yellow Robe will motivate them to write their own accounts.

Stew Magnusson said prior to the publication of his book *The Death of Raymond Yellow Thunder*, "If someone declines to read my book because I'm not Native American, then there's not much I can do about it."[2] I am not an Indian. That, in itself, might be an issue, but there have been other challenges or problems as well. I might as well address them now.

I pride myself on the thoroughness of my research. However, that research has often been frustrating in its own right. For example, in one census report, a person might be listed as Kate but then as Susan in another. There might be two children named Joseph in the same family. An oral historian on the Rosebud Reservation told me that it was quite common to reuse names, especially if one of the siblings died early in life. Census takers and recorders often exercised freedom or creativity in trying to convert Indian names to white names. The spellings of names often seem capricious—even in important matters. "Chauncey" is spelled in some records and articles as "Chauncy." Even his name on his tombstone is spelled without an "e." Dates of birth are elusive and inconsistent. For example, Chaucina Yellow Robe, the second of three Yellow Robe daughters, is documented in some sources as being born in 1908. However, the Social Security Master Death Index states that she was born in 1909. Both the federal and Indian census reports give her date of birth as 1910. And Chauncey's obituary in the *New York Times* in April 1930 states that she was 16—meaning that she would have been born in 1914.

There is the whole matter of family relationships. Terms used to describe European derived family relationships do not always apply. "Cousins" are not necessarily children of one's parents' siblings; "uncles"

Preface

might not be the siblings of one's parents or the parents of cousins at all. In some prominent Indian families adopted children claimed to carry on the lineage of their adoptive parents while lineal relationship might not be considered meaningful at all. Persons referred to as "grandmother" are not necessarily even related. In fact, one of the principal sources of information about the central character in this work—Chauncey Yellow Robe—demonstrates the different interpretation of grandmother. In the forward to *The Real Rosebud: The Triumph of a Lakota Woman* by Marjorie Weinberg, Luke Yellow Robe refers to "Grandmother Rosebud" and identifies himself in his salutation as "Rosebud's grandson."[3] Thereafter, countless websites and reviews about the book have referred to Luke as Rosebud's grandson without explaining that the term was not being used in the white European way, indicating that the person was the actual mother of one's parent. Luke Yellow Robe's great-grandfather was not Chauncey Yellow Robe. It is important to bear in mind the context of the relationship under consideration and to provide some clarification for the reader if necessary. The fact is that most of the "history" of American Indians has been heard and seen through the ears and eyes and written by the hands of white people. For Native Americans one person's truth is not always another person's truth, and we white people just do not always get that.

Another problem in researching the life of a famous person is to determine what is the truth, what is untrue, what has come to be accepted as the truth and that which, while not true, demonstrates an important characteristic of the subject. A person who is referred to as a "great chief" by family members or even in one book might not even be mentioned in another account. Sometimes it is difficult to separate the truth from the hype about the exploits of Chauncey Yellow Robe.

To overcome these research challenges, I have attempted to merge the available information from a multitude of sources with the oral history of people on Rosebud and others who are part of the extended Yellow Robe family. I have tried not to be dismissive about anything. I have limited my reliance on those things "written down" to the personal correspondence of key individuals and to printed and archival sources that address things that are not part of the accepted oral tradition. However, in some cases the written versions differ markedly from oral accounts and stories. I have chosen not to ignore it when those differences exist. I agree with Angela Cavendar Wilson, who said that "to truly gain a grasp of American Indian history, the other historians—tribal and family historians—must

Preface

be consulted about their own interpretations of and perspective on history,"[4] but I also realize that stories change with each telling and memories fade with age.

There is a great deal of new information about the Yellow Robes in this book. I have included information about his complicated participation in the Society of American Indians. I have explored his work history in detail. Not all of it will be embraced by his family or by others who have written about him. There are not any salacious or inflammatory revelations. Kills in the Woods (Chauncey) went to the Carlisle Indian School in 1883. In many ways he never fully left it or what it represented at the time. These things and others can be documented. Taken as a whole, I think that the reader will find Chauncey Yellow Robe's story to be illustrative, informative, interesting, and even intriguing.

Introduction

Outside the main gates of the Columbian Quadricentennial in Chicago throngs of people crowded into the bleachers at Buffalo Bill Cody's Wild West Show. They watched enthralled, as war painted savages made pretend war on innocent white settlers and the United States Army. Inside the gates of the White City, much smaller crowds listened politely as a handsome, articulate young Native American docent talked about the "miracle" that was the Carlisle Indian School. That young Indian, Chauncey Yellow Robe, innocuously was describing how the United States government was waging real cultural war on the nation's first people—his people. He came to Carlisle as a naïve young man who did not speak English and who had only recently seen his first white man. He experienced nearly unprecedented success there and was frequently put on exhibit as the face of the school and what it could accomplish. His appearance at the Columbian Quadri-Centennial and his participation as an interpreter at congressional hearings about the abuses Indians were suffering in the Wild West shows capitulated him into the national spotlight.

As he left Carlisle Chauncey had no way of knowing that he was already, figuratively, at the defining point in his life. Years later he railed against the abuses and negative stereotypes inherent in the Wild West show in national publications and in speeches. He appeared in a movie and two of his three daughters were in show business capitalizing on their "Indianness." He chose a profession that involved working for most of his adult life in government operated off-reservation boarding schools for Indians that were committed to "killing the Indian to save the man." At the same time he thought it was important to teach his "half-breed" daughters the stories and traditions he had learned as a youth as best he could remember them. He lived less than a half-day's journey from the reservation where he grew up and was enrolled there, but seldom visited reser-

Introduction

vations except to recruit or apprehend students who had run away from the school in Rapid City, South Dakota.

At the turn of the twentieth century, Native Americans seemed to have had limited options. The Indian wars were over, and the winner was clearly not them. They could follow the path blazed by Richard Pratt to assimilation, largely devoid of any remnants of their culture. They could take the path that led "back to the blanket" and reservation where they could live a life dependent on government subsidies. Or, for some, they could join the Wild West shows and tour the country and world as objects of curiosity and even nostalgia. It was in this milieu that Chauncey Yellow Robe emerged as an embodiment of the fact that assimilation, authenticity, Pan-Indianism, and even entertainment need not be mutually exclusive. In his introduction to the film *The Silent Enemy*, Chauncey implores the viewers to "look not upon us as actors." The film was to be a truthful depiction of Indian life. Perhaps Chauncey eventually learned that it was easier for him to be an Indian in the white man's world than an Indian on the reservation he had left.

Chauncey was an avid letter writer and regularly corresponded with Carlos Montezuma and many of the outstanding Native Americans of his day. His letters to William Pratt continued throughout their lives. Most of those letters were written on stationary bearing this monogram:

The symbolism is simple but striking. Badger Clark, South Dakota's one-time poet laureate, said that Chauncey Yellow Robe was a person who knew both worlds, and both worlds are represented in his stationary—the bow and arrow of his Indian world and the sophisticated font of the white world.

Chauncey Yellow Robe

Born a savage of the prairies,
　　Died a scholar of the hall,
Yellow Robe a strange tale carries
　　As he answers Wakan's call—
Memories of war and wages,
Death-songs and the talk of sages,
Flaunted scalps and printed pages,
　　With a drumbeat pulsing all.

Longer far the trail he covered
　　Than a white man ever saw.
Where the wild Sioux eagle hovered
　　With its bloody beak and claw
He began his march, and wended
　　Forty centuries that ended
Where Minerva's owl attended
　　Courts of learning and of law.

Smooth his manner when you scanned him,
　　Light his converse and urbane,
Yet a brooding hour would brand him
　　Ogallala of the plain,
As his face grew harder, colder,
Life a face carved on a boulder,
And his night-black eyes would smolder,
　　Like Sioux campfires in the rain.

Now he's left both hall and prairie,
　　And to me his goal is blurred.
Was it Heaven? Or the aerie
　　Of the mystic Thunderbird?
Well, although my thoughts may eddy,
Yellow Robes are calm and steady....
Having known two worlds already
　　He is good for any third.

—*Badger Clark, Hot Springs, South Dakota*[1]

1

Lakota Creation Story

This story was told to me by a Santee grandmother. A long time ago, a really long time when the world was still freshly made, Unktehi the water monster fought the people and caused a great flood. Perhaps the Great Spirit, Wakan Tanka, was angry with us for some reason. Maybe he let Unktehi win out because he wanted to make a better kind of human being.

Well, the waters got higher and higher. Finally, everything was flooded except the hill next to the place where the sacred red pipestone quarry lies today. The people climbed up there to save themselves, but it was no use. The water swept over that hill. Waves tumbled the rocks and pinnacles, smashing them down on the people. Everyone was killed, and all the blood jelled, making one big pool. The blood turned to pipestone and created the pipestone quarry, the grave of those ancient ones. That's why the pipe, made of that red rock, is so sacred to us. Its red bowl is the flesh and blood of our ancestors, its stem is the backbone of those people long dead, the smoke rising from it is their breath. I tell you, that pipe, that *chanunpa*, comes alive when used in a ceremony; you can feel power flowing from it.

Unktehi, the big water monster, was also turned to stone. Maybe Tunkshila, the Grandfather Spirit, punished her for making the flood. Her bones are in the Badlands now. Her back forms a long high ridge, and you can see her vertebrae sticking out in a great row of red and yellow rocks. I have seen them. It scared me when I was on that ridge, for I felt Unktehi. She was moving beneath me, wanting to topple me.

Well, when all the people were killed so many generations ago, one girl survived, a beautiful girl. It happened this way: When the water swept over the hill where they tried to seek refuge, a big spotted eagle, Wanblee Galeshka, swept down and let her grab hold of his feet. With her hanging on, he flew to the top of a tall tree which stood on the highest stone pinnacle in the Black Hills. That was the eagle's home. It became the only spot not covered with water. If the people had gotten up there, they would have survived, but it was a needle-like rock as smooth and steep as the skyscrapers you got now in the big cities. My grandfather told me that maybe the rock was not in the Black Hills; maybe it was Devil's Tower, as white men call it–that place in Wyoming. Both places are sacred.

Chauncey Yellow Robe

Wanblee kept that beautiful girl with him and made her his wife. There was a closer connection then between people and animals, so he could do it. The eagle's wife became pregnant and bore him twins, a boy and a girl. She was happy, and said: "Now we will have people again. *Washtay*, it is good." The children were born right there, on top of that cliff.

When the waters finally subsided, Wanblee helped the children and their mother down from his rock and put them on the earth, telling them: Be a nation, become a great Nation—the Lakota Oyate." The boy and girl grew up. He was the only man on earth, she the only woman of child-bearing age. They married; they had children. A nation was born.

So we are descended from the eagle. We are an eagle nation. That is good, something to be proud of, because the eagle is the wisest of birds. He is the Great Spirit's messenger; he is a great warrior. That is why we always wore the eagle plume, and still wear it. We are a great nation. It is I, Lame Deer, who said this.[1]

That great nation, the "Sioux," first encountered whites in the Mille Lacs region in Minnesota in the early 17th century. They lived on small game, deer, and wild rice. Faced with increasingly hostile and now armed enemies, they moved away from the lakes to the west and south—no doubt attracted by the abundance of buffalo.

After the coming of the horse around 1750, they stopped practicing farming and followed the buffalo as long and as far as the weather would allow. In cold weather, they trapped beaver. Hunting parties pushed farther into the west and their reputation as fierce warriors grew. Inevitability, they met with hostility, resistance, and encroachment as white settlers moved through and into their domain.

One of the first major confrontations took place near Fort Laramie, Wyoming, in 1854. A pattern of attack and retaliation followed for several years until a treaty was signed that gave the Indians possession of the Black Hills in perpetuity. The white interpretation of "in perpetuity" was quickly mitigated by the discovery of gold in the Black Hills, and like most treaties, it was not honored. In one of the subsequent conflicts, George Armstrong Custer and over 250 of his troops were killed at the battle of Greasy Grass, or the Little Bighorn, on June 25, 1876. Later the massacre of at least 200 men, women, and children by the U.S. Army at Wounded Knee in 1890 signaled the virtual end of Indian resistance. Reservation life became the norm.

The Rosebud Reservation is home to Sicangu Oyate, or Brule, one of the seven tribes of the Lakota nation. The Lakota have been seen traditionally

1. Lakota Creation Story

as the Native people who best represent the Plains Indian culture. They were known for their organized bands, charismatic leaders, dependence on the buffalo for food and virtually everything else, and for their involvement in warring.

Today the Lakota on the Pine Ridge and Rosebud Reservations have come to be viewed as representatives of the disastrously baneful effects of reservation life and white exploitation. Articles and reports from all over the world comment about the rate of alcoholism, suicide, joblessness, diabetes, and general hopelessness found there. Ironically, they are also at the epicenter of a rebirth of traditionalism, cultural restoration, and pride. Many of the most important events in the history of Native Americans have occurred in this area, and the Yellow Robe family has been part of the history of the Rosebud Reservation from its creation to the present.

Canowicakte (who became known as Chauncey) described the place where he lived, hunted, and fished as a child as "the plains of what are now North and South Dakota, Nebraska, Wyoming, and Montana."[2] At one time they knew no boundaries; now, over twenty thousand tribal members live on scarcely 1,900 square acres that make up the Rosebud Reservation's total area in south central South Dakota. The buffalo are on ranches, fishing is regulated, and the tipis have been replaced by mobile homes. But there are still Yellow Robes there.

They are the Sicangu Lakota Oyate or the Burnt Thigh Nation. That name probably originated after a prairie fire destroyed a Lakota village. Many people died, but those who could save themselves did so by running through the tall flaming grass to the safety of a nearby lake. The survivors were burned on their upper legs from their escape. While it might sound overly dramatic, altruistic, or philosophical to say it—the people on the reservation still carry those "scars" and are still getting burned. While trying not to sound condescending and further marginalize them, they are a people who, despite what has been done to them, are still proud, creative, honorable, and admirable. The Yellow Robes, on and off the reservation, are great examples of these qualities.

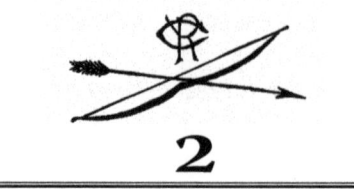

Pratt Comes Calling

It had been a long, tiring journey for Sarah Mather. They had traveled fifteen hundred miles by train, boat, and finally wagon. Each conveyance had brought its own unique and terrible form of sickness and discomfort. She was sixty-three years old and clearly too old for this kind of adventure, but when Captain Pratt told her what he was going to do, she had to go along. She would look after the girls. That was a lot different from what she had done at Fort Marion in St. Augustine. There, she had taught Pratt's Indian students, but this was going to be different. These new students, Lakota from the Rosebud and Pine Ridge Reservations, were young people—not prisoners of war in the strictest sense.

More than once, as she retched bouncing along in the back of the wagon, on the boat, or in the train, Sarah Mather had to have reflected on her own life and how she had come to be wherever it was that she was. Make no mistake about it, growing up in Northampton, Massachusetts, and having the last name Mather meant that religion played a big part of her life—like it or not. Intelligence, skepticism, and education were important as well. She was the great-great-great-grandniece of Cotton Mather, the famous Puritan minister, who was generally recognized not only as a theologian but also as one of the great intellects of his time. She was the daughter of William Mather and Annie Clark, both of whom were born during the same year as was the United States. In some ways Sarah was what many men feared most in her time—she was a smart, independent, free thinking woman who did not like being told what to do and how to live. After leaving Mount Holyoke College, she moved to Virginia and taught in private schools for fourteen years.

In 1857, she was introduced to the citizens of St. Augustine by O.M. Dorman, a prominent local attorney, and Miss Mather's School for Young Ladies was born. Later, Sarah and her longtime partner Rebecca Perit

2. Pratt Comes Calling

quickly became solidly entrenched in the city's social, political, and educational affairs. She taught wealthy young ladies, slaves, and later freedmen. Eventually she worked with Richard Pratt and the Florida Boys at Fort Marion. These "boys" were in actuality seventy-two prisoners taken by the United States Army after the conclusion of the Red River or Buffalo Wars of the southern plains. Clearly, Sarah Ann Mather believed in the transformative power of education, and that is why she was where she was. As soon as Pratt asked her to join him, she replied in a telegram, "I will go. How long before leaving?"[1] Pratt described her participation this way:

> Miss Mather, then sixty-three years of age, who had helped so loyally in the education of the prisoners in Florida, had urgently desired to accompany me to the Indian country if I again went after children. I could have no better assistant to help and take care of the girls, and I telegraphed her at St. Augustine, Florida, on September 8 that I was leaving for Dakota on the 10th and asked her to join me at Carlisle and go as an assistant to look after the girls. She came and we proceeded to the Rosebud Landing on the Mississippi River.... During the afternoon Miss Mather became wretchedly seasick and we had to stop several times.[2]

When Sarah Mather and Captain Richard Pratt reached Rosebud, they found that the Indian agent there, Cicero Newell, had already broached the topic of "recruiting" their young men and women to attend the Carlisle Indian School in Pennsylvania. The Indians were not impressed. Pratt reasoned that, "the agent's unfamiliarity with the pros and cons of the movement and the objections of the white employees at the agency against sending children so far away prompted the chiefs to decide that they would send no children."[3] Pratt insisted on speaking with them personally. Mather was there to help.

Speaking through an interpreter to a group of about forty that included the great leader Sinte Gleska, or Spotted Tail, as well as White Thunder, Milk, and Two Strike, all prominent chiefs, Pratt talked about the school and told them that he believed that the Indian young people were capable of learning as much as the white youth, and therefore could be their equals. For his own reasons, Spotted Tail agreed to send four of his sons and two of his grandchildren back to Carlisle with Pratt and Mather. Others followed his example, and 34 young people left Rosebud that day. The first group of "recruits" was carried east by wagon, boat and train. They reached the Carlisle Barracks in Pennsylvania in the middle

Chauncey Yellow Robe

of the night on October 6, 1879. Spotted Tail's support made the opening of Carlisle possible. Ironically, when he and several other leaders from the Plains tribes were brought to Carlisle the next year to celebrate the conclusion of the end of the first term, Spotted Tail demonstratively removed his sons and grandchildren and nearly destroyed the school and its reputation.

Pratt was not only a persuasive man, he was determined. He also believed that education could change lives and, in fact, he had proven to most to be an effective, albeit dogmatic, educator. Unlike many white people of his time, he seemed sometimes actually to like Indians. He just hated their culture and saw it as the only real obstacle to their assimilation. So, his job was clear. He would not only educate the Indians in basic academic and vocational skills, he would also eliminate that obstacle—even if, and more fundamentally because, it was necessary to "kill the Indian to save the man." Many more were to follow that first group to Carlisle. Kills in the Woods and his brother Search the Enemy, two of the sons of Tasinagi, were among them.

The story about the Yellow Robe family did not begin when these brothers arrived at Carlisle in 1883; nor did it end when Chauncey Yellow Robe (who arrived at Carlisle as Kills in the Woods), arguably the most

The student body at Carlisle assembled in front of Richard Pratt's quarters.

2. Pratt Comes Calling

well-known member of the family, died in 1930, shortly after completing one of the first reasonably authentic movies about North American Indians. Growing up in South Dakota and having the name Yellow Robe meant and continues to mean that being a Native American would play a very important part in one's life. Some of the family stayed on the Rosebud Reservation. Others moved away—some in both body and spirit. Regardless, the Yellow Robe family was, and still is, one that is full of individuals who possess extraordinary gifts, talents, intelligence, and stories that make them paradoxically both typical and atypical from Native Americans throughout history. Whether their history is written or transmitted orally, it is full of adventure, contradictions, accomplishments, disappointments, and mystery.

When Canowicakte, or Kills in the Woods, retraced Sarah Mather's path toward Carlisle, he did not do it with the clarity of purpose and strong sense of self that she possessed. He might be starting a great and exciting journey, or someone might be taking him to the edge of the world to toss him off—he really did not know. All he knew was that he was the son of a man named Yellow Robe, the son of a woman who was said to be the niece of Sitting Bull, and a product of the Plains and the indigenous people who lived there.

3

Canowicakte's Early Life

Canowicakte, Kill in the Woods, or Chauncey Yellow Robe, was born sometime around 1870 in the southern part of what became the state of Montana. Exact birth dates are often impossible to determine, and probably not all that important, but different sources give his date of birth variously from 1867 to 1870. The 1870s are generally referred to as the last decade of the buffalo, and life on the prairie was about to change dramatically. In *The American Indian Magazine,* Chauncey described his naming ceremony.

> When I was still an infant, my father and mother gave a big feast to the chiefs, warriors and medicine men of the tribe in my honor and brought me before them. They named me Canowicakte, meaning kill in woods, and allowed one of the chiefs to pierce both of my ears with a sharp instrument, and my father gave away two of his ponies. This signified that I would have the right to wear ear rings.[1]

Canowicakte spent his youth running, playing, hunting, fishing, chasing buffaloes, and listening to his grandparents relate the stories, beliefs, and values that he was expected to learn, remember and pass on to his children. Canowicakte called his grandparents "my tutors in legends."[2] The legends were *woyake,* spoken for just that purpose—to be passed on.

As a young man, he learned to listen and learn about *Waka-tanka*—the Great Mystery or the Great Spirit. He learned about the Sun Dance and how it honored *Wi,* the Sun, who was part of the complicated and multi-dimensional *Waka-tanka.* He learned the importance of focusing inward and listening to the voices of the *wanagi*—those spirits or "ghosts" of everybody and everything that had once been alive. He also learned to listen to *He Sapa,* the wind, and he learned to hear, through the music

3. Canowicakte's Early Life

and prayers of his people, how to reproduce that voice as closely as possible. He experienced the extremes of life on the prairie—the scarcities of *waniyeth* or the winter, and the abundance of early summer. He saw his grandmother and other women teach the children how to find *timpsula*, or prairie turnips—a dietary staple whose leaves seemed to direct its hunters by pointing to the next plant. He learned about and saw the ever-present nearness of death. His grandfather, or *T'ukasila*, explained the death and birth of all things as *hocokat'uya*—all things take place in a circle. To all of these lessons, as a child, all Canowicakte could say was *slol waye sni*—of these things I know nothing.

Canowicakte was getting more than a little frustrated. What had started out as a short walk into the woods in the bottomlands near the river had turned into an hour-long trek in the snow. The winters in the northern plains were severe, but today it was just cold. He had marked the sapling in late summer. It was an ash—straight and about as thick as a man's wrist. Grandfather had said that a young oak would be all right, but it was clear to Canowicakte that his grandfather thought ash was better. So, when they found just the right one, he marked it by tying a small piece of cloth in its limbs. Now he could not find it. His name meant "kill in the woods," but today he was just wandering around in the woods. Then he saw it. Canowicakte cut it and took it back to his grandfather's lodge.

There his grandfather quickly peeled off the bark and started to work. Using a draw knife, he split the sapling. Canowicakte knew that sometimes his grandfather could actually produce two bows from the same piece of wood—but not this time. Using the knife and a rasp, he shaped the cut side of the bow into a form with which he was eventually satisfied. Then he built a fire outside and suspended the bow above it. There it would dry for several hours. After that he removed the bow and started the long process of shaping and testing. Canowicakte lost count of the number of times he shaped then tested the bow for flexibility. Slowly the bow developed an elegant shape that looked almost perfect to Canowicakte who was getting somewhat impatient. Still his grandfather shaved the bow, bent it, and shaved some more. Finally, and just as the seven-year-old Canowicakte had reached the end of his patience, grandfather declared the bow to be ready, but not ready to be shot. Canowicakt was shown how to draw the bow back smoothly and evenly. He continued to practice. He would draw, aim, and release, but used no arrows and shot no game.

Such was his early life in the northern plains. He watched, he learned,

Chauncey Yellow Robe

and he grew. It was probably this same bow that he took with him on his first buffalo hunt a few years later—an account he detailed in "My Boyhood Days." This encounter was a seminal event in his life. At that time Canowicakte was living with his aunt and uncle—Iron Plume and manage to slip away to join the hunt. Although he admitted to being afraid at first, his training as a hunter and horseman gave him the confidence to fell a yearling buffalo. The days of the great buffalo hunts were coming to an end. Canowicakte lamented, "My people did not kill buffalo or other game for pleasure. They only killed for use; but the white man came and killed them off for sport."[3]

Political boundaries had little meaning for a young Native American at that time, but the territory that "belonged" to the Sioux Nation had already started to dwindle and would do so even more before Canowicakte had any real concept of what a reservation was. He defined where he lived in broader terms—determined by where buffalo hunting and warfare led his people. Both of those activities were in the process of changing drastically. Increasingly, white people—settlers and migrants—were moving into and through the area. It was not just that the massive buffalo herds were being eliminated. All the while, what he had come to see as his way of life was changing and was about to implode.

The exact number of siblings Chauncey had is open to questions. Chauncey's father had several wives and numerous children. One thing is certain ... he had a large family. One indication of the size of his family is that he had a sister whose name was Plenty Brothers. Canowicakte's younger brother, Search the Enemy, had spent most of his life with his uncle, which was common for an Indian boy. They had narrowly avoided a bloody encounter with Custer's troops at Greasy Grass Creek when he was only about five years old. Search the Enemy's life no doubt pretty much followed the same watch-listen-learn pattern that Canowicakte's did until he returned to the Rosebud Reservation in 1883.

Representatives from the Carlisle Indian Institute were making their yearly "recruiting" trip to Rosebud, and this time, their father decided that Canowicakte and Search the Enemy should go with this man named Pratt to the "apple land" in the east. They were obedient and respectful sons, and so they agreed to go. Search the Enemy later said that "so one day I told my father to go see them if they could take us to the school ... and oh, I was glad because he (Pratt) had no objection and selected us."[4]

Canowicakte later said that it was certainly against his wishes that

3. Canowicakte's Early Life

he went. He said that on that day his "dreams for glory in the Indian world vanished from my vision. Against my own wishes I was given to General R.H. Pratt to take to school in the far east."[5] The irony of these initial positions soon became obvious. Canowicakte's modern day relatives commonly state that he bravely volunteered to go to Carlisle in order to prevent his other brothers from having to go. This position seems groundless in light of the fact that another brother did, in fact, go at the same time and that Search the Enemy seemed more willing than Canowicakte. Attendance at Carlisle certainly was not forced on them. Other on-reservation day schools and a boarding school were viable options for the Yellow Robe family.

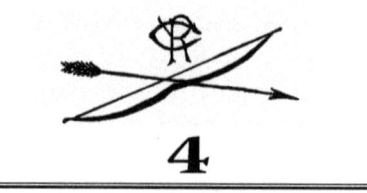

4

Clothes, Hair and Names

Just a few years before he and his brother were turned over to General Pratt, Canowicakte saw his first white man. Chauncey's daughter, Evelyn Finkbeiner, said that he was about twelve years old at the time. His family was camped outside a trading post on the Missouri River when a strange creature with long hair, wearing a large hat, and carrying a musket walked toward him and his brother. Convinced that he was seeing an evil spirit he ran to his father leaving his brother behind. According to Canowicakte, his father identified the creature as a white man and warned him that they should "not go very far or the white man would kidnap us."[1] On that day in November 1883, as they boarded the train and took their seats in what Ota Kte (Luther Standing Bear) called those "little houses standing on long pieces of iron which stretched away as far as we could see," he probably felt that that warning had come true. Like hundreds of other young Indian children, the young men who later became known as Richard Yellow Robe, and Chauncey Yellow Robe had noteworthy experience.

As the train lunged forward, most of the fifty Indian children grabbed hold of the seats and held their blankets between their teeth in near horror. They were dressed in the regular "Indian" clothes appropriate for that time of the year. Some of the older children had warned the young ones not to lean to the left or right for fear of causing the train car to tip over. Word had been spread that they were heading toward the land where the sun rose where they would probably be thrown over the edge by angry white people. At stops along the way they were greeted by white people who pressed their faces against the train windows to get a better look and were mocked with "war whoops." They were expected to eat food that they did not recognize with utensils they had no experiences using. Their

4. Clothes, Hair and Names

usual response was to wrap the food that they could in their blankets and eat it later.

Canowicakte said that on the way east he "wore my full Indian costume, long hair, not knowing a word of English, not having seen a book or a school house before."[2] So, essentially these young Indians were traveling to a place that was unknown to them, supervised by people who spoke a different language and were perhaps even evil spirits, for a purpose of which they were unclear. The adult recollections of Standing Bear and Yellow Robe, while frightening, probably do not come close to recounting the sum total of the fears these children felt at the time. It is important to remember that these experiences were being replicated throughout Indian Country as the off-reservation boarding school became the federal government's Indian education model of choice.

After several days in transit they arrived in Carlisle, Pennsylvania, during the night of November 20, 1883. Some sources give the date as November 14. The new students walked the two miles between the train station and the school. Then, instead of being allowed to fall off the edge of the world or being pushed off, Canowicakte was told to sit in front of a mysterious strange black box along with his brother and an Indian boy who came to be known as Henry Standing Bear. After what seemed like an interminably long time of looking at the box and not knowing what to expect, they hear a faint click and then were sent on their way. General Pratt had adopted the practice of having the school's photographer, J.N. Choate, take pictures of the new students as they arrived as savages in order to be able to show the radical transformation that took place as evidenced in the "after" photographs.

The most famous of these was the twinned pictures of Tom Torlino, a young Navaho man. However, Canowicakte's "before" picture of Chauncey was cropped from the original picture of the three young Indians and paired with his "after" picture to adorn the cover of the school's 1895 catalog. Having served the public relations purpose of establishing just how barbaric the Indian youth were, their clothes were then taken away and their hair was cut. It was one of the first invasions on Indian culture done at Carlisle.

What David Wallace Adams describes as a "two front assault on Indian children's cultural identity" had begun.[3] Ostensibly to control the problem of head lice and in the interest of cleanliness, the hair cutting and disposal of traditional clothing was a necessary part of stripping the

Left: Three young Brule students upon arrival at Carlisle Indian School in 1883. After names were given or chosen, they became known as (from left) Richard Yellow Robe, Henry Standing Bear, and Chauncey Yellow Robe. *Right:* The same three students (from left), Chauncey Yellow Robe, Henry Standing Bear, and Richard Yellow Robe. The before-and after-photography was a favorite practice at the school to emphasize the immediate impact of "Americanization" (both courtesy Archives and Special Collections, Dickinson College, Carlisle, Pennsylvania).

children of the outward manifestations of their culture. Canowicakte thought that perhaps his mother had died and that his hair, and that of the other students, was being cut as an outward sign of grief. Others, at other times, were so resentful of this particular intrusion that revolts or near-revolts took place. Canowicakte's homesickness was palpable. Later he came to appreciate the white people at Carlisle. Not a feeling shared by many other students there.

The immediate hair cutting was instituted at Carlisle and then expanded to other agencies and jurisdictions. Commissioner of Indian

4. Clothes, Hair and Names

Affairs William Atkinson Jones sent this letter to superintendents of all federal reservations and agencies in January 1902. The notorious missive soon became known as the "haircut order." He was especially concerned that students who were returning to the reservations after boarding school might go "back to the blanket." He said it this way.

> The wearing of long hair by the male population of your agency is not in keeping with the advancement they are making, or will soon be expected to make, in civilization. The wearing of short hair by the males will be a great step in advance and will certainly hasten their progress towards civilization. The returned male student far too frequently goes back to the reservation and falls into old customs of letting hair grow long. He also paints profusely and adopts all the old habits and customs which his education in our industrial schools has tried to eradicate.

Commissioner Jones advocated extreme measures that might induce compliance to this expectation.

> With you Indian employees and those Indians who draw rations and supplies it should be an easy matter, as a non-compliance with this order may be made a reason for discharge (if employed in the Indian Service) or for withholding rations and supplies ... the returned students who do not comply voluntarily should be dealt with summarily. Employment, supplies, etc., should be withdrawn until they do comply and if they become obstreperous about the matter a short confinement in the guard-house at hard labor, with short hair, should furnish a cure.[4]

Clearly Commissioner Jones felt that "killing the Indian" simply would not work if he or she were reborn or resurrected on the reservation.

At the boarding school, after being thoroughly bathed and stripped of their clothing (most of which would be priceless today) they were given the official Carlisle uniforms. Boys were dressed in sharp looking military-like uniforms, and the girls were fitted with the prescribed Victorian style dresses. While attractive and functional, these forms of dress were sometimes seen as demeaning and most often remarkably uncomfortable by the students.

On the third day at Carlisle one of the most extraordinary and arbitrary assaults on their culture took place. New names were given. While practices varied at different times and at different places, the general rule was to accept the white interpretation of the Indian child's father's name (remember that most Indians were matrilineal) and attach a fairly common European first name to it. Often, with the assistance of translators, the

Chauncey Yellow Robe

Indian children were allowed to choose their first names from a list written on the chalkboard. The general lack of understanding or concern about Indian names gave rise to capricious and ethnocentric practices.

Frank Terry, the Superintendent of the boarding school for Crow Indians in Montana, wrote about naming practices in the boarding schools.

> The system of proper names in vogue in America and in certain of the European states is, as we believe, well devised. It is so simple as scarcely to occasion remark. The name of some prominent ancestor gone, and, in most cases, forgotten, is handed down from generation to generation of his posterity, and each child, at birth receives this, through the operations of laws written and unwritten, as his surname. The parents place before this one or more names especially pleasing to them as the child's Christian name, and his designation is thereby rendered complete. It is a good system, for it fixes the name of each individual after an unvarying fashion, and establishes the same practically beyond alteration. We are so accustomed to it from our youth up that it seems to us perfectly natural that it should be so. We cannot see how it could be otherwise than as it is. Furthermore, and what makes it more important, it is practically the only system known to American law, and it is impossible not to see that in all things, prominent among which is the transfer of property or the bequeathing of the same to heirs, trouble must come to those who disregard this system.
>
> This system of nomenclature the government of the United States in its dealings with the Indian tribes has aimed to establish among them as one means the better to fit them for the privileges and advantages of American citizenship; and that this is a wise and humane act on the part of the government cannot be gainsaid. The Indian Department has continually urged this matter upon its agents, superintendents, and other workers "in the field." The command to give names to the Indians and to establish the same as far as possible by continuous use has been a part of the "Rules and Regulations" for years past.

Dr. W.N. Hailmann, General Superintendent of Indian Schools issued additional regulations which applied to Indian youth who were enrolled in the government schools:

> ... Indian agents and superintendents of Indian schools have not sought to impress the Indian people with the importance of having their names fashioned after the whites, consequently they have had in this direction the opposition instead of the co-operation of the Indians. In this thing, as in nearly all others, the Indians do not know what is best for them. They can't see that our system has any advantages over their own, and they have fought stubbornly against the innovation. Furthermore, these officials have not exercised due care to discover or select the correct family names, or when selected have not made sufficient effort to fix those names upon the members of the respective families.

The regulations and directives were not without attempts at what the white writers thought was funny.

4. Clothes, Hair and Names

A funny little incident is reported from the Apache reservation in Arizona. An Indian policeman rode up to the government school and delivered a little boy to the superintendent. "What's his name?" inquired the superintendent. "Des-to-dah," replied the Indian in Federal blue, as he rode away. "Destodah," mused the superintendent. "Queer name, ain't it? 'Max' will fit him very nicely for a 'first name.'" So the little fellow was duly christened "Max Destodah." It turned out, however, that des-to-dah was the Indian word for "don't know." The policeman had simply said he didn't know what the boy's name was. It further turned out that Max was one of four brothers in the same school, no two of whom had the same surname. One finds many cases here and there where a name is not carried through the family.

Attempts by white people to translate Indian names proved to be problematic.

> Translations of Indian names, as a rule, have been unsatisfactory, though there are exceptions. The case is reported from the Pawnee reservation, Oklahoma, of an Indian name Coo-rux ruh-rah-ruk-koo. He was commonly called Afraid-of-a-bear. The literal interpretation of his name, as given to me, is "fearing a bear that is wild." With this interpretation the agent proceeded to call the Indian Fearing B. Wilde; not a bad arrangement, if he had made a success of it. But he did not, for the allotment was finally made to the Indian's native name. But such names as Flying eagle, Pipe-chief, Crazy-horse, Yellow bonnet, Afraid-of-his-enemy, Walk-in-the-water, Rain-in-the-face, Bull-all-the-time, Keeps-his-head-above-water, No-hair-on-his-tail, Bob-tail-wolf-No. 3, Kills the-one-with-the-blue-mark-in-the-centre-of-the-chin, are ridiculous and should not be perpetuated. Such names are uncouth, un–American, and uncivilized.

The government's bottom line about Indian names became apparent.

> Hence it will be seen that the Indian names are nothing, a delusion, and a snare, and the practice of converting them into English appears eminently unwise. It is certain that the name on the rolls at the agency is the interpretation of only one of the Indian's several "names." A short Indian name in their own vernacular, or a syllable or two of a long one, if euphonious and pronounceable, as they usually are, will answer quite well for a family name, but the translations are never satisfactory, and cannot be too strongly condemned.[5]

I am completely aware that I probably have already tested the patience of the reader far too long with the length of that last article, but the practice of naming, and more importantly, the mindset involved in that practice, is important to understand. Indian naming practices were as arbitrary as assigning names to African American slaves that indicated their owner's rather than their actual names.

As the last visible vestiges of their traditional culture seemed to be

Chauncey Yellow Robe

disappearing, Search the Enemy made his choice of names and became Richard Yellow Robe, and Kills in the Woods made his and became Chauncey Yellow Robe. He might have chosen that name because it was somewhat like Canowicakte or Chano as he was sometimes called. He might have chosen it because it sounded French and reminded him of the first white people he had met—French traders. In this manner, wonderfully colorful, expressive, and meaningful names like Whirlwind Soldier, Little Bear, Lone Wolf, Spotted Eagle, Like-the-Bear, Afraid of His Horses, and Yellow Robe were linked to names like Tom, Susan, Luther, Mary, Walter, and Don. In some cases, Indian names that translated poorly into English were dropped altogether and new surnames simply created.

The Yellow Robe name itself is of questionable origin even among family members. If you enter the words "yellow robe" into any internet search engine, thousands of entries will come up. Most deal with what might appear to be a fairly simple question like, "Why do certain Buddhist monks wear yellow robes?" One answer is that in ancient India the color yellow became associated with renunciation because it was the color of tree leaves about to fall in autumn. Some answers could be more practical, functional, or even ironic. For example, yellow was the color that was most readily available in natural dyes, and it did not show the dust as badly as other colors. A few entries will deal with a prominent Native American family. Fewer still will even try to address the question, "How did the Yellow Robe family acquire that name?" Even among the few answers there is little consistency or agreement. Like so many things, it simply depends on who you ask or what you read.

One answer to that question was that the name Yellow Robe was taken by White Thunder or Tasinagi, Chauncey Yellow Robe's father and a Lakota, after a battle with Crow Indians. According to this version, the Lakota fought a band of Crow who had taken several horses from their camp. Yellow Robe, a Crow chief, realizing their inevitable defeat, asked the Lakota to spare his ten-year-old son who had accompanied him on the raid and to raise him in their tribe. As he finished his plea, White Thunder felled him with an arrow to the heart. After the fighting was over, the body of the young dead boy was discovered. In response, White Thunder then assumed the name Yellow Robe as a tribute to the Crow's bravery.

Another version holds that the Crow and Lakota agreed to settle a longstanding dispute about hunting rights in the Yellowstone area by

4. Clothes, Hair and Names

having a brave from each tribe fight to the death, with the victor's tribe getting exclusive hunting rights. White Thunder and Yellow Robe fought with White Thunder emerging as the winner. In tribute to the fallen warrior, White Thunder took his name with the promise to carry it forever. While it is certainly true that the Lakota naming traditions and rituals permitted the occasional but purposeful changing of one's adult name, it is doubtful and unsupported that assuming the name of a chief of a hereditary enemy for any reason would have been part of that complicated belief and tradition system.

Quoting Luther Standing Bear, James Curiel states that "In Lakota, Nakota, and Dakota societies the main considerations were meanings, honoring a relative, physical and mental characteristics, tribal symbols, totems, religious symbols, nature, phonetic aesthetics, and acts of bravery. Lakota, Nakota, and Dakota naming practices were complex, highly personalized choices conveying identity, personal history, family history, special talents, and attributes."[6]

Significantly, in this statement, acts of bravery were not extended to include those of other individuals, and certainly not enemies. In *My People the Sioux*, Luther Standing Bear talked about how he acquired his name. He was given initially a simple, birth order name and then had the name *Ota Kte* or Plenty Kill bestowed upon him by his father after he killed his first bird while hunting with his uncles and cousins.[7] Other accounts suggest that his father had killed many enemies. Still later, Plenty Kills became Standing Bear. In any event, Lakota like Standing Bear often had as many as three names—one of which was equivalent to what we might call a nickname.

The aforementioned accounts of how the name Yellow Robe came into being are generally held and provided by members and descendants of Chauncey's immediate family and were attributed to stories that he told his children. There just does not seem to be any basis for it other than those stories; but in a culture where oral history is so vitally important, to most that just might be enough. Certainly the mere act of a white person writing a particular version down does not legitimize or delegitimize it, In fact, having something chronicled through a white person's eyes and ears often distorts the truth.

There is at least one other straightforward explanation. In this version, there was still a battle; there was still a Crow warrior chief named Yellow Robe; and there was still a young son of that Crow. The Crow

Chauncey Yellow Robe

Yellow Robe was killed in that battle, and his son was taken by the Lakota, but that son was Tasinagi himself or perhaps his father. This explanation is given some credence by the fact that Yellow Robe was a common name among the Assiniboine or Stone Sioux, the Northern Cheyenne, and, most significantly, the Crow. All of these tribes lived in Montana, which was organized as a territory in 1864 and became the 41st state to be admitted into the Union on November 8, 1889. Both Tasinagi and Chauncey gave the place of their birth as Montana. Some present day descendants still consider the Crow Yellow Robes relatives and comment about the family resemblance.

The name itself follows one of the patterns described by Oneroad and Skinner in that it includes one noun modified by one adjective.[8] The use of the color yellow was also significant. It has been described variously as a color preferred by the spirits, the symbolic color of the Wakinyan, the color of the shaman's tipi indicating that he has spoken to the great god Inyan, and even the color of the face and body paint worn by a warrior who has honorably killed an enemy.

So, there is also a very real possibility that no promise was ever made to perpetuate a name forever in memoriam. Tasinagi might have become Yellow Robe because he distinguished himself in battle, and his own valor earned him the name. Even Chauncey, in his "My Boyhood Days," only talks about his father in terms of being a "fearless warrior, runner, and great hunter," and does not mention the naming incident.[9] As in the case of the yellow robes of the Buddhist monks, the simplest and most practical explanation might be the best one.

5

Killing the Indian

As bad as they were, haircuts and name changes were just parts of a more comprehensive plan to "kill the Indian." Native languages had to be eliminated, and Native belief systems had to be eradicated. For these things, the real process of cultural assault—the educational program at Carlisle—was about to begin.

In Pratt's mind the difference between being a savage and being a civilized person was determined by one's environment. To become civilized it was necessary to eradicate one environment and replace it with another.

> It is a great mistake to think that the Indian is born an inevitable savage. He is born a blank, like all the rest of us. Left in the surroundings of savagery, he grows to possess a savage language, superstition, and life. We, left in the surroundings of civilization, grow to possess a civilized language, life, and purpose. Transfer the infant white to the savage surroundings, he will grow to possess a savage language, superstition, and habit. Transfer the savage-born infant to the surroundings of civilization, and he will grow to possess a civilized language and habit. These results have been established over and over again beyond all question; and it is also well established that those advanced in life, even to maturity, of either class, lose already acquired qualities belonging to the side of their birth, and gradually take on those of the side to which they have been transferred.[1]

The kind of education that he saw as necessary to do that would contain a few basic elements. In 1908 R.H. Pratt repeated a pronouncement he had made in 1892.

The kind of education that will end the Indian problem, by saving the Indian to material usefulness and good citizenship, is made up of four separate and distinct parts, in their order of value as follows:

> First: Usable knowledge of the language of the country.
> Second: Skill in some civilized industry that will enable successful competition.

Third: Courage of civilization which will enable abandonment of the tribe and successful living among civilized people.
Fourth: Knowledge of books, or education, so-called.
In justice to itself the government can have but one aim in all it may do for the Indians, and that is to transform them into worthy, productive American citizens. The vital question is, can the material be made to yield the desired product?[2]

In fairness to Pratt, it must be pointed out that he could answer his own question affirmatively. In fairness to thousands of American Indian children, it must be pointed out that Pratt's model of education did irreparable harm to most of the students who were caught in the emotional and cultural battle that emphasized "killing the Indian to save the man."

The operative slogan at Carlisle would always be: "To civilize the Indian, get him into civilization. To keep him civilized, let him stay."[3] Pratt thought he knew how to accomplish that. The plan and program were fairly simple and straightforward. Pratt was convinced that it had worked with the "Florida boys" at Fort Marion and that it would work with Indian children at Carlisle. They would spend roughly one-half of the day in the classroom working on basic academic skills—primarily learning to speak, read, and write English, and the other half learning and working at various vocational programs such as telegraphy, business studies, carpentry, tailoring, tinsmithing, printing, baking, sewing, or farming.

Perhaps the most important part of the education at Carlisle was the "outing" program. In this program students spend different amounts of time working for individuals, families, and companies in the surrounding communities. Pratt saw this as the ultimate "Americanizer." Outing was so important Pratt called it Carlisle's "right arm."[4] Students would learn basic values; they would have to learn to use the language operationally and in a variety of different settings; and they would see the various complexities, subtleties, and nuances that comprised civilized life. The outing experiences were initially limited to the summer months and involved the careful placement of students in neighboring households. Later they evolved into longer term experiences, sometimes being a year or two of immersion, and some were placed in industrial or mercantile settings. During these year-or-more outings, the Indian students attended the public schools in the counties where they were placed. As it turned out, more often than not, especially in the beginning, the boys worked on farms and

5. Killing the Indian

the girls worked in the houses with household chores and childcare. According to Pratt:

> the outing program accomplished a number of things. It fostered the acquisition of English by forcing students to apply their new-found language skills in practical work and family settings. It broke down prejudice: Indians came to appreciate the goodwill of their white patrons, while patrons gained an increased appreciation of the Indians' capabilities. Students learned the subtleties of civilized living, the little nuances of speech and behavior that could never be fully acquired in the superficial atmosphere of school.

Pratt also argued that the outing system gave Carlisle students the "courage of civilization."[5]

Working with and alongside Pratt was A.J. Standing. Standing had a long history of working in and for Indian education. He had established a school among the Kiowa in 1874 and was one of the first people Pratt contacted to work at Carlisle. Standing was also a strong proponent of outing. The Commissioner of Indian Affairs spoke glowingly about the practice of outing at Carlisle in his annual report to the Secretary of the Interior.

> Some of the eastern training schools have adopted a system known as "outing," which in my judgment is an important auxiliary in educating Indian youth and preparing them for self-support. It is notably carried on at the Carlisle school, which, without disparaging other Indian training schools, may be said to stand in the front rank, if it is not the foremost, of institutions engaged in the great work of Indian education.
>
> This system consists in placing out for a series of months among the families of farmers in that part of Pennsylvania, boys and girls who have had a year or so of training at Carlisle, and can make the most of the advantages thus afforded them for learning practical farming, the use of tools, and thrifty housekeeping....
>
> In some cases, they remain a year at these places, attending district schools in the winter. Such a training upon a farm is the best possible way of fitting them for the ownership and cultivation of the lands which are being allotted them by the Government. This experience, taken in connection with their training and education at school, places them beyond all reasonable doubt upon a footing of self-support.[6]

Clearly the outing program was designed not only to do what he said but also to provide prolonged periods of time for the Indian children to soak up white civilization. It also provided a way to prevent any gaps of time that might normally result in an inclination to want to return home.

All was not perfect for Pratt and Carlisle. Early in the history of the

Chauncey Yellow Robe

school Spotted Tail became concerned that the school was far too militaristic and removed his children. This single act came close to destroying the school. Pratt was committed to the military model and stated that it "taught them obedience and cleanliness, and (had) given them a better carriage."[7] Apparently, it also angered and confused others because significant numbers of children ran away. "Runaways plagued the authorities at Carlisle. If students were caught and brought back, they were punished by being locked in the guardhouse."[8] Nearly half of the students who were dismissed or sent home from the school were runners. Others who might be considered troublemakers or malcontents were simply dropped because their period of "enrollment had expired." Richard Yellow Robe was one of these students. Chauncey, on the other hand, not only survived—he thrived in this environment.

The program of study at Carlisle emphasized the learning of the English language. In the first year, students were presented with pictures of objects and then told the English word for it. They then repeated that word. Eventually they would be shown the proper spelling of the word. They would write or trace over lightly written letters or words until they learned them. From there they would move on to reading and writing simple sentences. The school catalog said that "the most important work of the lower grades is to teach the correct use of the English language."

Like most students, Chauncey spoke no English at all upon entering Carlisle. Not unlike today's emphasis on reading across the curriculum, the catalog goes on to say that during the intermediate years, the use of reading and language "correlates with the lessons in industry, geography, nature study, literature, and morals and manners. The aim in elementary reading is to train the pupils so that they may be able to find independently the thought expressed in written or printed words, in order that they may eventually turn to books for knowledge, pleasure, and inspiration."[9]

The scope of mathematics instruction began with primary attention being given to mental exercise, accuracy, and neatness to practical application and problem solving in the secondary years. The catalog concludes the discussion of math this way: "The aim is to make the study of this subject less an operation of figuring and more of thinking; a study not of processes, but the use of them."[10]

The science program emphasized the study of nature, geography, physiology, and hygiene. The curriculum evolved or dissolved into a

5. Killing the Indian

vocational program. In 1910, school superintendent Moses Friedman, the in the section of the catalog dedicated to "purpose" said:

> It is the aim of Carlisle to train the Indian youth of both sexes to take upon themselves the duties of citizenship. Indian young men and young women are given thorough academic and industrial training, which prepares them to earn a living, either among their own people or away from the reservation in competition with whites. It is primarily a vocational school for both sexes. Its graduates and ex-students are engaged as efficient workers and leaders among their own people on the reservation, and as teachers and officials in the government service, and are successfully competing with whites, away from the reservation, in the trades and professions.[11]

Friedman himself became the object of an investigation by the Secretary of the Interior. He was generally recognized as being both incompetent and universally disliked. Among the more substantiated claims was that renowned football coach Glen (Pop) Warner was the real leader of the school and that athletic success had come to be the most important feature of the school. There were several nasty cases of excessive corporal punishment that came to light. Cleanliness, grounds maintenance, hygiene and health, morale, and academic standards had all suffered immeasurable and perhaps irreparable damage. Friedman was removed from the position. However, during Chauncey's time at Carlisle, there was no question about who was in charge; that made the decisions; and what the focus of the program was to be. It was Pratt's school, Pratt's program, and Pratt's obsession. Ironically, a self-professed shy Indian boy who came to Carlisle, like so many others, distrustful of white people became an important part of Pratt's school, and his role grew steadily during his time there.

In *The Real Rosebud: The Triumph of a Lakota Woman*, Marjorie Weinberg says that Chauncey stood out early and that his "earnestness, sincerity, and gentleness, combined with a keen sense of humor, attracted Pratt's attention."[12] Pratt's attention and admiration increased during a school camping trip in which Chauncey displayed a willingness and eagerness to do whatever was necessary and in the best interest of the campers. Apparently they shared a love of fishing as well. Like Jacqueline Fear-Segal points out in *White Man's Club*,[13] it might be tempting, but very problematic to suggest that Pratt's interest in Chauncey was exploitative or self-serving, despite the carefully manufactured and cropped images used on the catalog. They developed a legitimate and close relationship while at Carlisle that lasted for years, despite not agreeing on the racial aspects of Native Americanism.

Chauncey Yellow Robe

If Pratt viewed outing as the "right arm" of the school and as the "supreme Americanizer,"[14] it is easy to see how Chauncey's success in it not only reinforced his opinion but also contributed to his high opinion about Chauncey. As mentioned previously, initially this experience for boys meant working on a farm. Whenever possible, Pratt placed students with Quaker families who had proven to be generally supportive of his efforts. From Chauncey's first placement with Lewellyn Fries in Solebury, Pennsylvania, in 1885, his evaluations were all excellent. In March of 1886, he was placed with Mr. William B. Sutton in Lahaska, also in Bucks County. He received an excellent evaluation there as well. His other outings included placements with D.S. Mershon on Morrisville and S. Barber in Harrisburg. Richard, on the other hand, did not fare so well. On August 16, 1887, he was dismissed as a result of running away from an outing placement in New Hope.[15] By this time, both young Yellow Robe men had established their own unique pattern of behavior, and by mid-summer of 1891 while Chauncey was distinguishing himself as a stellar student, Richard had left the school. Chauncey was beginning to take a place on the national stage; Richard returned to Rosebud where he would "die" *before* enlisting in the armed forces.

Chauncey Yellow Robe as a new student at Carlisle. Cropping of pictures, taken primarily by the school's photographer, J.N. Choate, was frequently done to highlight or spotlight certain students. These photographs frequently appeared in the school's promotional materials, catalogs, etc. (courtesy Archives and Special Collections, Dickinson College, Carlisle, Pennsylvania).

The November 21, 1890, edition of *The Indian Helper* reported that "Chauncey Yellow Robe has been to Wash-

5. Killing the Indian

ington on a short visit, where he interpreted at the examination made in the Indian office of the Indians traveling with Buffalo Bill. Acting Commissioner Belt wrote to Pratt about Chauncey: "'We thank you for sending so capable an interpreter as Yellow Robe was found to be.'"[16] This investigation took place as a result of numerous complaints about abuse of Native Americans who were part of Buffalo Bill Cody's traveling Wild West show. The previous year a new Commissioner of Indian Affairs had taken office. Thomas Jefferson Morgan immediately expressed his disdain for the employment of American Indians in the wild west shows. In an interview with a reporter he said that the way Indians were being represented in these shows, with their war dances, war paint, etc., was blatantly misleading. Commissioner Morgan directed the Indian agents to give their immediate attention to the issue and to report to him:

> First. The names of each and every Indian who has been connected with these shows at any time during the last five years, giving the name, age, sex, and condition, how long absent, and with whom. If still absent let that fact appear. (He was not averse to taking away these Indian's allotments, yearly annuities, or even tribal status.)
> Second. What manner of life those persons are living who have returned to the Agency.
> Third. What their influence is, so far as you are able to gather it, upon those with whom they associate.
> Fourth. What the health is of those who had returned, as well as what diseases they have brought back with them. On these points, I desire that you will have a careful inquiry made by the physician at your Agency, and that you will submit with your own report his official report concerning the matter. What in your judgment should the Government do about such shows?[17]

Newspapers had been reporting alleged wild west show abuses of American Indians for several years and continued to do so. The *Wheeling Register* reported:

> Five red Americans of the Dakota tribe of Sioux, who have been assisting Buffalo Bill, got here yesterday on the steamship Saale. They came in the steerage with a lot of foreigners. One of them, a tall, little-limbed buck of 18, was so ill that General O'Beirne, who is an old plainsman and understands the Sioux language, had him sent to Bellevue Hospital. His right arm from the wrist to the elbow is badly ulcerated. The arm, according to the hospital surgeon who examined it, looks as if it had been broken and not properly attended to. It gave the young Indian great pain, which he bore with smiling stoicism. Besides this ailment he has consumption. His name is Kill His Pony. None of the Indians looked as if they had had an altogether pleasant time abroad. All but Kill His

Pony, who probably will never come out of Bellevue alive, start tomorrow to join their tribe at Pine Ridge Agency. Kill His Pony had a severe hemorrhage just after landing at the barge office.[18]

An article in *The Washington Post* said

The condition and complaints of ill-treatment made by the Indians who have recently returned from Buffalo Bill's and other shows now in Europe has been set forth in a letter sent by Gen. James O'Beirne to Thomas J. Morgan, Commissioner of Indian Affairs, at Washington. General O'Beirne points out the violation of the contracts made by Cody and other managers, and suggests that an investigation be made by the United States authorities.[19]

The Aberdeen (SD) *American News* carried a story reporting that

Painted Horse, one of the Indians from the Red Cloud agency who was with Dr. Carver's show in Europe, arrived here Saturday on the steamer *Augusta Victoria*. Today in the presence of General O'Bierne he made a long statement in which he charged both Carver and Buffalo Bill with great cruelty toward the Indians under their charge. Painted Horse said he was repeatedly tied up until he could endure no further suffering. He was fed upon "stinking meat" and other things wholly unfit for food; his money was taken from him and when he asked its return he received only $5. He said other Indians were also shamefully treated and were repeatedly fired upon with both blank and ball cartridges and badly wounded. They were permitted to have all the whiskey they wanted and when under its influence they often fought among themselves. Gen. O'Bierne has a copy of the agreement entered into by the Carver combination in which good treatment to the Indians is specified particularly as one of the conditions of their engagement. A copy of Painted Horse's statement will be prepared and forwarded to the secretary of the Interior and to the Indian commissioners. According to the latest advices Buffalo Bill's Indians will arrive in Philadelphia next Thursday.[20]

This type of story was repeated in most major newspapers of the time. Buffalo Bill Cody hired literally hundreds of "show Indians" to perform in his exhibitions and travelling shows, despite repeated allegations by social reformers and Bureau of Indian Affairs officials that the show mistreated, exploited, and misrepresented the Indians. In the final analysis, Thomas J. Morgan, Commissioner of Indian Affairs could do very little, and the American public continued to be ravenous consumers of a misrepresented Indian culture for several more years.

Not all Native Americans felt demeaned or abused by the shows and their organizers. In the same hearings where Yellow Robe was an interpreter, Acting Commissioner Robert V. Belt directly asked the "show Indians"

5. Killing the Indian

there if they had been mistreated in any way. "All answered that they had not." One performer, Rocky Bear said, "If the great father wants me to stop, I would do it. That is the way I get money. If a man goes to work in some other place and goes back with money, he has some for his children."[21] Chauncey obviously took exception to that opinion. This hearing piqued his interest and fired his passion. These hearings, coupled with other, more personal experiences, resulted in Chauncey becoming more than an interpreter. By 1914 he added his own articulate voice and words to the outrage.

After he returned from his job in Washington, and as he was preparing for his more prominent appearance at the Chicago World's Fair, Chauncey had to deal with the issue of his brother, Richard's, "death." Student Clarence White Thunder returned from a visit to Rosebud in 1892 with the disturbing news that Richard had died. According to White Thunder, the source of the terrible news was none other than Richard's father.[22] Clarence, an 1897 graduate, went on to become, as did several Carlisle graduates, a teacher in an Indian school. What was surely a distraction to Chauncey remains somewhat of a mystery. Richard, having left Carlisle on July 2, 1891, returned to Rosebud to enlist in the armed forces. The "mystery" is exacerbated by a document that indicates that Richard actually did enlist in the army on December 19, 1891.[23] However, in 1892, Richard was listed as an employee of the Indian Service working at Rosebud.[24] Most sources say that the evidence indicates that he died in 1893. His name appears on the 1892 Indian Census of Rosebud. He is listed as being twenty-three years old.[25] So the reports of Richard's death, though premature, were rather prophetic. There is no evidence that points to a health condition or life-style that would cause such a misunderstanding, and the role of Chauncey's father in it still not clear. There are still other related Yellow Robe mysteries to come.

6

Chauncey in the White City

In 1893, the world came to Chicago, and Chicago presented itself to the world. The Columbian Quadricentennial was supposed to begin in 1892, but the enormity of the project forced a delay. During the World's Columbian Exposition visitors, exhibitors, vendors, and just plain folk descended on the White City on the banks of Lake Michigan. The Carlisle Indian School participated in the opening parade and continued having a presence during the fair. Rosebud Yellow Robe said that Chauncey was "chosen to represent the North American Indians at the Congress of Nations opening of the World's Columbian Exposition,"[1] and in fact, Chauncey did address the Congress. In that speech he talked about the importance of education for the Indians and the necessity of having that done in schools that were off-reservation.

The Indians will never be led "through the paths of civilization and education" if the school he attends is placed at the door of the tepee. (Chauncey borrowed the phrase "through the paths of civilization and education" from Democratic President Grover Cleveland's Second Inaugural Address on Sunday, March 4, 1893. Cleveland said: Our relations with the Indians located within our border impose upon us responsibilities we cannot escape. Humanity and consistency require us to treat them with forbearance and in our dealings with them to honestly and considerately regard their rights and interests. Every effort should be made to lead them, through the paths of civilization and education, to self- supporting and independent citizenship. In the meantime, as the nation's wards, they should be promptly defended against the cupidity of designing men and shielded from every influence or temptation that retards their advancement.[2] What he needs most is to get beyond the atmosphere of

6. Chauncey in the White City

the reservation. We shall have to cut loose from the old life, if we are ever to put on the new.

> When I left the reservation in South Dakota, I had positive knowledge of some of my tribal brothers, who attended reservation schools, and there are none who have been able to rise above their surroundings and attain to an independent manhood. Break up the reservations, abolish the rations system, make our education compulsory, and the conditions for making men will then be more favorable than if every reservation had a dozen schools within its limits.[3]

Pratt described Chauncey's role at the fair this way, "One of our foremost pupils, Chauncey Yellow Robe, who came in the first party of students, a fine specimen of gentlemanly young manhood, was part of the exhibit as a sample and to assist in giving information."[4] He might well have added that he was a fine specimen who could be counted on to say the right thing at the right time.

Not altogether unexpectedly, the fair itself, or more specifically, the representation of the American Indian at the fair became contentious. Some, like Pratt intended to show "how the Indian could learn to march in line with America as a very part of it, head up, eyes front, where he could see his glorious future of manly competition in citizenship and be on an equality as an individual. (While the) exhibit contrived by the two government bureaus was calculated to keep the nation's attention and the Indian's energies fixed upon his valueless past, through the spectacular aboriginal housing, dressing, and curio employments it instituted."[5] He was referring to the Indian Bureau and to the Ethnological Bureau. Emma Sickles, who had originally been part of the Midway Project, which planned all of the exhibits, protested so vehemently that the director of the project, Frederick Ward Putnam, professor of anthropology at Harvard's Peabody Institute, dismissed her. In an article in the *New York Times* she wrote:

> Every effort has been put forth to make the Indian exhibit mislead the American People. It has been used to work up sentiment against the Indian by showing that he is either savage or can be educated only by government agencies. This would strengthen the power of everything that has been "working" against the Indian for years. Every means was used to keep the self-civilized Indians out of the Fair. The Indian agents and their backers knew well that if the civilized Indians got a representation in the Fair the public would wake-up to the capabilities of the Indian for self-government and realize that all they needed was to be left alone.[6]

Chauncey Yellow Robe

While Pratt could not agree totally with Sickles, he felt that the same misrepresentation that she saw as an impediment to self-government and independence was an obstacle to his goal of complete assimilation. The government's portrayal of the savage, even the noble savage, coupled with the fact that Buffalo Bill's Wild West Show, while not formally a part of the fair, occupied a prime location near the main entrance, essentially determined how fair visitors would feel about Indians as they left. The fair that brought the United States the Ferris Wheel, Cracker Jacks, the hamburger, Juicy Fruit gum, breakfast foods like Quaker Oats, cream of wheat, and shredded wheat was also the venue where Frederick Jackson Turner delivered his "The Significance of the Frontier in American History" thesis which essentially declared that the American frontier was closed. The disagreements and differences of opinion about how best to deal with the continent's aboriginal inhabitants did not end with the frontier. The Chicago Fair took place only three years after the massacre at Wounded Knee, and that aspect of the frontier was far from closed.

Chauncey's observations and reflections while he was in Chicago for the fair were frequently printed in *The Indian Helper*, one of Carlisle's publications. Then, as now, visitors were concerned about the weather. The fair opened to the public on May 1 and closed on October 30, 1893. Whether Chicago got the nickname the "Windy City" from its infinite number of verbose politicians who lobbied for its selection as the host city, or from the soothing breeze that came off Lake Michigan in the summer, cooling visitors might be open for debate. However, what is not open to much debate is the fact that Chicago can be hot in the summer and can get very cold in October. Chauncey reported back to Carlisle that it really did not make any difference. Visitors continued to pour in come, whether the weather was good or bad, hot or cold.[7]

On more than one occasion while he was in Chicago, Chauncey must have thought about the first time he came to Sotoju Otun Wake, or the Smoky City on his way to Carlisle; about how he had looked to the west and dreamed that his parents would come to rescue him; and about how far he had come and how much his life had changed since that day.

Yellow Robe fully embraced his responsibilities as a docent at the exhibit and not only represented the school well, as Pratt knew he would, but also took advantage of the opportunity to further broaden his horizons. He visited and revisited the various exhibits, demonstrations, and programs whenever possible. He reported that "when I first came, I walked

6. Chauncey in the White City

hastily through the buildings and saw how big and beautiful they were but there was so much I could not understand, it made me tired to look, and I did not see much. But now," he says, "I'm beginning to see and learn and understand."[8]

His wanderings probably took him down the midway to "Omaha Charlie" Bristol's Indian relic show and exhibit where over 500 pieces of Indian artifacts, taken from the corpses of massacred and mutilated Ghost Dancers only a couple of years before, were displayed. The most prized display was that of the body of an Indian infant dried and placed in a glass box. The "mummified papoose" was a major draw. He might have even stepped outside the fairgrounds to see Buffalo Bill's Wild West Show. These events played significant roles in his maturation.

Probably Chauncey was only incidentally aware of the extent of the controversy about the representation of Indians at the fair and was almost certainly unaware the Carlisle exhibit deliberately had been placed in as inconspicuous place as possible. In February 1895, he wrote an essay about the fair: "It may be truly said that the World's Columbian Exposition was the most successful gathering that had ever been held upon this continent; and greater than any other exposition held in this or any century ... it was a wonderful manifestation of man's power." The subtleties and undercurrents of certain aspects of the event were not lost on him: "Buffalo Bill's Wild West Show (that) has simply degraded and demoralized the Indians is allowed by the United States Government. Such exhibitions as that will never turn the Indians toward the light."[9] While in Chicago, he made contacts and established relationships that would in a few short years lead to his significant participation in a national Indian advocacy organization.

Chauncey's life at Carlisle involved more than being the face of the school at important events. General Pratt was more than willing to take him and other exemplars to meetings, churches, and conferences whenever possible. His daughter Rosebud indicated that he played football while at Carlisle, but he played long before football became the school's obsession. In fact, Pratt sought to ban football being played against teams from other schools because it was violent and dangerous. Since, Carlisle's first sanctioned team played its first full season in 1894 it is unlikely that Chauncey got caught up in the football fever that eventually infected Carlisle. Chauncey won the indoor 100 yard race in March of 1891.[10] His extracurricular pursuits were not all athletic; he was assistant secretary for the Standard Debating Society.[11]

Chauncey Yellow Robe

Much like Charles Eastman, Henry Roe Cloud, Carlos Montezuma, and other young Indian men being educated in the east, Chauncey attended the Northfield Student Conference of Young Men's Christian Associations hosted by Dwight L. Moody at his school in Northfield, Massachusetts. This conference was held during June and July while most students were not in school. The conference idea was generated by Moody and Luther Wishard who was the Secretary of the Young Men's Christian Association at a meeting in 1885. The idea was to hold an annual Bible study program for undergraduate men. The next year over two hundred and fifty students from eighty-nine schools, mostly colleges and universities, met for twenty-six days at Mount Hermon. The next year it was moved to Northfield. The morning sessions were devoted to missionary and Bible study classes while afternoons were given over to recreation and sports. The morning session ended with a "sermon," and there were sunset and evening messages as well.

From the moment in 1883 that the newly named Chauncey Yellow Robe decided to get in the line at Carlisle that was for Indian children who had decided that they were going to be Episcopalians, his education on and off campus contained a strong religious component. Chauncey had no idea what the tenets of the Episcopal Church were at that time—he couldn't even read or speak English. He simply went in the direction that most of

Chauncey Yellow Robe (left) and his father, Tsainagi. "Going back to the blanket" was never a consideration for Chauncey.

6. Chauncey in the White City

the other children seemed to be going. While he did not choose the ministry or mission work as an occupation, it did enter his mind for a while. Although he did not express it like Carlos Montezuma, Chauncey's real "missionary" work would be directed toward the white world.

Pratt seemed to view religious instruction as important but subordinate to the main purpose of civilizing or "citizenizing" the young Indians. It was important to purge them of the old rituals and beliefs, and, in that sense, Christianity was seen as something that might solidify or create a unity of thought or belief and not "save souls." In *Education for Extinction*, Adams expressed it this way: "Embracing Christianity meant embracing an entire ethical code which included among other things, the principle that an individual was responsible for both his economic and spiritual self."[12] No doubt many Indian children were converted to active Christianity; some probably went along with the program without really accepting it; and an untold number probably continued to practice their traditional beliefs and rituals secretly.

7

Thriving in an Unlikely Environment

Carlisle School has been credited as being the vanguard of cultural genocide. There really cannot be much disagreement with that. It was the federal government's prototype for off-reservation boarding schools. Its curriculum metastasized throughout the boarding school system of schools. Fear-Segal writes that

> he (Pratt) dedicated the Carlisle Indian School to a dual mission. First, to eradicate native tribal cultures and instruct Indians in white ways to equip them for citizenship in the United States; second, to demonstrate to white Americans that this transformation was both possible and desirable, Pratt spent the next twenty-five years shaping, nurturing, expanding, and commanding the Carlisle Indian School as well as defending its program and philosophy. The school was a living experiment, which became a monument to him and the mission he championed.[1]

David Wallace Adams said that "the boarding school, whether on or off the reservation was the institutional manifestation of the government's determination to completely restructure the Indians' minds and personalities."[2]

Coleman, in *American Indians at School, 1850–1930*, writes that "the assimilationist vision and energy of Captain (later general) Richard Henry Pratt triggered the large-scale move to off-reservation boarding schools."[3] Records and stories about the boarding schools are replete with evidence of mistreatment, health concerns, unbridled corporal punishment, runaways, and even deaths of Indian children while at school. Carlisle was probably better than most, and the quality varied considerably between schools. Through today's eyes we can clearly see the deprivation, racism, and general inhumanity that were present. Recently a Native American friend was looking at the famous picture of the Carlisle students posed in front of Pratt's house. He described their eyes as empty, hollow, hopeless, and even dead. If Pratt's goal was complete cultural genocide, one need

7. Thriving in an Unlikely Environment

look no farther than the creation of the Society of American Indians in 1911, the resultant "pan–Indianism," and the role Indian school graduates played in them to see how that failed.

David Treuer has written that "as destructive as boarding school might have been, many Indians actually enjoyed their time there and had no unpleasant experiences."[4] There can be no doubt that the boarding school experience did irreparable damage to individuals. Historical or cultural trauma does exist in the Indian population. Some students were able to endure, exist, and return home relatively unscathed. Inexplicably, some, like Chauncey Yellow Robe thrived. His friendship with Pratt grew stronger, and he began a lifetime of work in Indian School Service boarding schools. The remarkable fact is that during 1899, the Office of Indian Affairs reported that American Indians comprised 45 percent of those employed by the Indian School Service. This startling figure reveals a neglected dimension of the United States assimilationist policy toward Indian peoples. Not only did the Office of Indian Affairs push for land in severalty and education, but it brought American Indians into the agency most responsible for transforming their cultures, the Indian School Service.[5] During the period between 1888 and 1899 the Indian School Service grew, but the proportion of Indians in the Service actually grew more. Then, as now, the reasons for choosing this type of government work vary, but for the most part they were either materialistic—a fairly good income, or altruistic—or want to do something for the benefit of their people. These Indians decided to become change agents in the community in which they work while not abandoning traditions and culture. So, ironically, the government was undermining the assimilation process by hiring the very people they thought would personify and perpetuate it.

Interestingly, Carlisle never considered itself or represented itself to be a college. In fact, in 1910, Principal M. Friedman, admitted that Carlisle was "a vocational school. It is neither a college or a university."[6] In the 1912 catalog, it presented a summary or record of its living graduates: 209 graduates were working on reservations; 85 were working for the Indian Service. Of that group, 40 were instructors and 20 were disciplinarians or field matrons. In that listing Chauncey was listed as a1895 graduate who was a teacher with the Indian Service at the Rapid City Indian School in South Dakota—not far from where he grew up on the Rosebud Reservation.[7] When he graduated, he was a confident, trusting, and articulate young man destined to succeed.

8

A Demented Indian

On November 3, 1895, the headline in the *Atlanta Constitution* screamed out

> A DEMENTED INDIAN
> Yellow Robe Is Still Locked Up For Safe Keeping.
> HIS CONDITION IS PITIFUL
> The Third Ranking Sioux Chief Is a Mental and Physical Wreck[1]

It was at the Indian Village during the Atlanta Cotton States Exposition. This time the world had been invited to meet the "New South," and just barely a month before the headline, Booker T. Washington, on September 18, 1895, had delivered his famous Atlanta Compromise speech. On October 17, Buffalo Bill and his extravaganza had rolled into town for a two week engagement. Apparently both the New South and the world still could not get enough of the American Indians. Indian trader Charles Philander Jordan had received permission from the Office of Indian Affairs to bring Indians ("warriors, squaws, and papooses") from the Rosebud Reservation to be part of the fair in Atlanta.[2] Jordan's permission was noted in the *Annual Report of the Commissioner of Indian Affairs, for the Year 1895*.

> March 9, 1895 (permission was granted) to Charles P. Jordan, licensed trader at Rosebud Agency. S. Dak., to take about 20 indians (sic) from the Rosebud Agency, for the purpose of exhibiting a Sioux Indian Village at the Atlanta Exposition.
>
> He had previously had charge of a party of Indians at the Midwinter Exposition in California, and in view of his good care and satisfactory treatment of those Indians, his personal acquaintance with the Rosebud Sioux, and his long connection with the Indian service, he was granted this special permission and no bond was required of him.[3]

Among the Indians were "several of the most noted chiefs of the Sioux nation. Some of the scarred red veterans (who) raided and fought with

8. A Demented Indian

Sitting Bull and took part in that famous massacre in which the gallant Custer and his command were wiped out on the Little Big Horn."[4] (The fact that Sitting Bull did not fight at all seems to have been of little consequence to the reporter). The Indian Village proved to be an extremely popular attraction. It was promoted as the only show that had been endorsed by the United States Government. The manager of the Village, M.F. Chamberlain, who had operated the one at the Chicago Exposition, said that it would be larger and more varied than the one at the world's fair. Now, the rest of the "Demented Indian" story as told in the *Constitution*:

> Yellow Robe, the demented Indian chief, is still at police headquarters, being held there for safekeeping. He is considered dangerous by the Indian village concessionaires at the exposition.
> The Indian was locked up several days ago, his brother Indians at the exposition fearing that he would do harm if left at the Indian village. He showed unmistakable signs of being demented and irresponsible, and it was thought best to deprive him of his liberty.
> The Indian in his right mind was a fellow absolutely harmless, the march of civilization having long since subdued the savagery of his nature. He looked upon the white man as his friend and protector and even extends his hand in friendly greeting to whites while he raves at the sight of his own countrymen. His nature is kindly and he is one exception to the proverbial saying that the only good Indian is a dead Indian.
> Yellow Robe's condition is pitiful in the extreme. Behind the iron bars of his cell at police headquarters he peers at a visitor in the most pathetic manner. His eyes are sunken and the unmistakable signs of time and care are depicted in the lines on his face. His features are expressive of the sadness that must be in his once proud heart. His mind wanders and he passes the time in restless pace to and fro in his cell. The Indian is almost a physical wreck, which adds to the hopeless condition which he is in.
> Yellow Robe is a famous Sioux Indian chief. He is the third ranking Chief of the Sioux tribes located on one of the government's reservations. He stands high in the councils of his native countrymen, and on the prairies he is known far and wide. He took part in many western campaigns and won for himself among the redskin braves an illustrious reputation for bravery and daring. In his younger days he was foremost in the war campaigns of his tribe and there was no more braver man who roamed the prairies.
> Yellow Robe is about sixty-five years old. He is bent with the troubles of time and his life is drawing to a close. He has a family, a wife and several sons in the far west. He has two young daughters in the Indian Village on the Midway, and it is said that his current mental condition is partly due to worry about his children.

Chauncey Yellow Robe

One of his sons in the west came near losing his life by accident two or three weeks ago and is now dangerously ill. It is said that when Yellow Robe heard of the accident and his son's condition, he at once lost control of his mind, the news giving him much trouble. He is said to be an Indian of exceptional regard for his family. And it is said that his daughters at the Indian village have given him cause for worry.

Yellow Robe and his tribe of Indians have a vast tract of country set apart for them in South Dakota. The tribe is located in what is known as the Rosebud agency in that state. The reservation is said to be one of the finest in the country. All of the Indians on the Midway came from the Rosebud agency. As stated Yellow Robe is the third ranking chief among his tribe. The first and second chiefs in rank are at the village on the Mid. The tribe is commanded by Two Strike, one of the most famous Indians in the Sioux nation. The second ranking chief is Stands and Looks Back. He is also at the village.

Yellow Robe was conspicuous in the ghost dance war, one of the most cruel in the history of the country. He took a leading part in that war and also in the great war against the Crow Indians. He was a brave fighter and until age broke him down he stood as one of the leading redskin braves in the country.

The Indian chiefs rank according to bravery and record. Two Strike is seventy-eight years old and Stands and Looks Back is fifty-five years old.

It is the intention of the Indians at the Midway village to send Yellow Robe back to his western home, there to end his days. Just when he will be sent west is not known is not known. His mental and physical condition would make a trip to the west dangerous for him now. He is under the care of Dr. N.O. Harris.[5]

In trying to determine who this particular Yellow Robe really was, a couple of different avenues have been followed. The supporting evidence in the article has been reviewed. Two Strike was a chief of the Brule Sioux. His date of birth has been given variously from 1815 to 1832. He was probably better known and appreciated among his people than among the whites. He did not claim the infamously high reputation of Sitting Bull or Crazy Horse; however, he was greatly admired and respected among the Sichanghu.

Stands and Looks Back or *Hakikta Najin* was born around 1851. So, at the time of the Cotton States Exposition he was approximately the same age as reported in the article. He was Oglala but lived most of his life on Rosebud. He holds the distinction of being one of the most frequently photographed Indians of his time.

Dr. N.O. Harris was a well-known and respected Atlanta doctor. He was an officer in the Atlanta Society of Medicine, and had testified in court regarding cases of mental competency. If, as the article, says, Yellow Robe

8. A Demented Indian

was "about sixty-five" years old, his date of birth would have been around 1830. Marjorie Weinberg gives the date of Chauncey's father as during 1826–27.[6] He would have been sixty-nine or seventy when the incident took place. The 1895 Indian Census of Rosebud lists him as seventy years old, and he was the only person with just the name "Yellow Robe" listed.[7]

Yellow Robe (White Thunder or Tasinagi) had at least three wives. "His first wife Thasina (Her Robe) bore him three children but died young. He then married Chauncey's mother (called Slow Bear in the census report but always referred to by Chauncey as Tachawin, who bore him seven children, and her sister Grabbing Bear or Catch Bear, who bore him eight children."[8] (One living descendent maintains that all of Yellow Robe's wives were sisters and all nieces of Sitting Bull.) All of the Yellow Robe descendants, and most references to him, refer to him as a chief, and most call him an important chief.

Finally, there is no other option. Tasinagi, by all accounts, was the first Yellow Robe among the Sioux. There were no others, especially no other chief, until he married and started producing other Yellow Robes. Circumstantial evidence points to the conclusion that the "demented Indian" in the Atlanta jail was the original Yellow Robe. His concern about his son's health harkens back to the previously reported "death" of Richard. When asked about the article and the Yellow Robe talked about it in, a relative dismissed the idea that it was Chauncey's father by saying that he was "too much of a traditionalist" to have been involved in the Indian midway exhibit. Traditionalism, in itself, did not prevent many Indians from participating in this and similar events. Two Strike and Stands and Looks Back were probably traditionalists as well, but their presence at the exposition is well-documented. The Official Catalogue of the Cotton States and International Exposition makes only one brief reference to the Sioux who were part of the exhibit. "Especially conspicuous are the Sioux chieftain, in full war paint, mounted on his gaily housed pony, and with feathered headdress sweeping to the ground; while facing him is a group of Kiowa Indians engaged in moving their habitation."[9]

Participation in one of the wild west shows is nothing to conceal or to be embarrassed about. Sitting Bull himself toured with Buffalo Bill in 1885, and even the Bedonkohe Apache warrior Geronimo sold autographed pictures of himself for a quarter at the St. Louis World's Fair in 1904.

9

The Indian Service School System

Chauncey Yellow Robe began working in the Indian Service School System shortly after graduating from Carlisle. During the five years after graduation, he worked at several different Service schools. The first position for which there are definitive records was at Genoa, where he began working in June 1895. Weinberg and others say that his first assignment was actually at Sisseton, South Dakota. While this employment is not reflected in the Annual Report of The Commissioner of Indian Affairs, it should be noted that beginning with the 1900 Annual Report and in subsequent reports, his starting date with the School Service is listed as April 1, 1895. His assignment at Sisseton could have been temporary from April until June. If, in fact, he was at Sisseton at this time, he would not have found conditions to be ideal. The Indian agent there reported that:

> The Government Boarding school for the past year did not prove satisfactory to me or the Indians, and it will take several years to overcome the mismanagement of the past year. I expected much at the beginning of the year, but was sadly disappointed. The school proved a complete failure, not only in health, learning, discipline, and general conduct of the pupils, but the expense of conducting the same exceeded any previous year.[1]

Things at Genoa were not any better.

The Genoa Indian Industrial School opened on February 20, 1884, in Nance County, Nebraska, on the grounds of an earlier vocational training school for Indian children. Located in the Loup River valley, it was the fourth non-reservation boarding institution established by the Office of Indian Affairs. Genoa and six other schools were founded while Henry Teller was the head of the Department of Interior. Despite Pratt's apprehension and opposition to his appointment, Teller's view of the schools

9. The Indian Service School System

as an economically feasible way of ending the "Indian Problem" resulted in the enrollment in Indian schools more than doubling during his administration. The town of Genoa was chosen because the Federal Government already owned the former Pawnee Reservation headquarters which was located there. Mormon missionaries founded Genoa town in 1857. It was one of several settlements that the Church of Jesus Christ of Latter Day Saints had established to serve as way stations for the Brigham Young Express and Carrying Company, which had the government mail contract to Salt Lake City. These stations also served as rest and supply stops for believers traveling across the Plains to Salt Lake City.

In 1859, the government forced the Mormons to abandon Genoa when the settlement became part of the Pawnee Indian Reservation. Genoa served as the Pawnee Indian Agency until 1876, when the Pawnee were removed to the Indian Territory, and the reservation lands became available for other uses by the federal government. The local citizens actually collected money and contributed $500.00 to the government to help it buy addition land for the institute.

The students who eventually came to the Genoa Indian School were from 10 states and over 20 tribes. In 1889 enrollment at Genoa was 175. Of those enrolled, Sioux children predominated with 101.[2] The Genoa Indian School, referred to sometimes as the Grant Institute, featured a basic curriculum, and was in most ways a replication of Carlisle. The primary academic concern was teaching the students English. Instruction level was determined by ability rather than age, and reading, writing, arithmetic were the curricular mainstays. Half of the day was spent in class and the other half in assigned trades. Genoa lacked the strong academic reputation some of the other schools had, but it was not without its admirers. In the June 5, 1891, edition of the school newspaper, *The Pipe of Peace*, a "Brief but Bright 'Write-up'" by the Big Brother of the *Columbus Sentinel* was published.

> It is worth a two-days' journey on horse-back to visit the Institute and take observations of the methods employed to rear the bronzed-faced children of the noble red man in the arts of civilization. Many of our readers have visited this school, but those who have not might be interested in knowing something concerning it ... it has come to be generally accepted among statesmen and philanthropists, and it has come to be the generally accepted belief that "education" is the only humane solution, and, moreover, it is cheaper than any other method of dealing with the scattered remnants of our aboriginal brethren. To accomplish this purpose eleven educational institutions have been established

and are maintained at government expense, the largest is at Carlisle, Pa. The school at Genoa is third in importance and bids fair to rank first within a very short time, having advantages of location and healthful surroundings not possessed by any of the others.

... Last Monday through the courtesy of Supt. Backus the *Sentinel* was permitted the freedom of the premises and noted with pleasure the perfect system upon which the school is conducted in its educational and industrial departments. In the first place, the utmost order and neatness prevails throughout the entire institution, and perfect discipline is maintained. The different departments of the school are under the immediate supervision of competent instructors, and many students show wonderful proficiency in their studies. The industrial departments, which are very important in the matter of fitting the boys for useful avocations, are something of a wonder, and to show what they amount to it is only necessary to state that in the past year the harness shop turned out 170 sets of the best double harnesses and 185 common. The broom factory shows a record of 1,000 dozen floor brooms and 100 dozen whisk brooms, all the work of Indian boys. The shoe shop produced 297 pairs of assorted shoes and did a large amount of repairing besides. The tailor lads made 76 complete suits of clothes, 270 pairs of pants, 145 coats, and 24 heavy aprons for the school, besides several suits for outsiders. A wagon and blacksmith shop is also entitled to notice, as the boys have just completed the first wagon, which will bear the most critical inspection. ... Much more of interest could be written concerning this school and the peculiarities of the pupils, but space forbids. But we venture the prediction that if the loyal and untiring efforts of Supt. W.B. Backus count for what they are worth, Grant Institute will, in a short time, be at the head of the Indian Industrial schools of America.[3]

Another article written at the end of July in *The Pipe of Peace* reported that it (Genoa) was "among the most important schools of its class in the United States, or for that matter perhaps in the world, ranking third in attendance but second to none in the active and effective part it is taking in solving the much mooted 'Indian question.'"[4] It is obvious that at Genoa, the answer to the Indian question involved the elimination of native language, assimilation into the white culture, and learning a viable trade. As these articles show, the primary pursuits of the school were vocational in nature, but recreation and sports played a part as well. Genoa competed interscholastically in several areas including debate, tennis, boys and girl's basketball, football, and baseball. Additionally ice skating was popular. The school had a well-developed intramural program as well, and entertained students by occasional trips to the circus.

The glowing editorial from *The Sentinel* notwithstanding, it is obvious that Genoa, like other boarding schools, had its share of problems

9. The Indian Service School System

and issues—perhaps more. The school attempted an "outing" program very loosely patterned after General Pratt's at Carlisle in Pennsylvania. Designed to assist Native American students in becoming more acquainted with white culture through direct contacts, at Genoa the program seemed to be more concerned with providing laborers for farmers in the area as well as for providing house servants in the city. The school found itself embroiled in a labor dispute with competing beet growers in Colorado when it appeared that they were going to "out" several students to help with the harvest there. The school received a meager $167.00 per student per year for support. Consequentially, much of what the school came to be about was to supplement their operating funds. This was done by selling the surplus from their gardens and dairy, participating in open commerce with the community through other industrial endeavors, the direct hiring out of labor, and most unfortunately, in cutting as many costs as possible.

Sanitary conditions at Genoa improved dramatically during the first year while Chauncey worked there. In 1895, the Genoa Town Company started providing the school with water. Before that, their source was a well operated by a windmill that pumped water into a 300 gallon storage tank. From there it flowed to the kitchens and washrooms in the school—the same facilities the superintendent admitted in his annual report of 1891 could stand some improvement. Communicable diseases became common and epidemics spread through the school almost yearly. Measles killed ten in 1892. Tuberculosis was also common and frequently deadly. Twenty-three students died of TB between 1884 and 1894.

Chauncey was hired as a disciplinarian at Genoa, although some relatives prefer to refer to him as a counselor. Like at other such schools, runaways were common. One of Chauncey's successors at Genoa was dismissed from his position because of the brutal way he dealt with runaways. "The school disciplinarian tied two captured runaways boy to a buggy axle, and a third boy was tied around the waist and driven ahead of the team of horses."[5] Atrocities and tragedies were far too common as desperate children took desperate risks in their efforts to escape. Accidents, such as falling off trains are reported from most schools. During his tenure at Rapid City, Chauncey would be directly involved in several recovery trips. Yellow Robe was hired at the school despite the fact that he lacked teaching credentials, training, or a college degree. These were not required for Indian School employment until 1928.

The superintendent at Genoa in 1895 was J.E. Ross. In an uncommon move for a government official, he indicated, in his 1895 annual report, that there were some problems at the school. In an all too common move for a government official, he attributed them to his predecessors. The enrollment was low. The buildings were in need of repair. He said that "the needs of the school are many, for owing to the numerous changes that have taken place during the past two years, no interest whatever has been taken as to the general welfare of the school."[6]

Apparently fires were a problem because he expressed his appreciation to the Genoa Town Department for providing ample fire protection "which we have been in a situation to appreciate during the past year," and a following message in The Genoa Leader for several weeks during December 1895.[7] There beside advertisements for Hood's Sarsaparilla, Dr. Kay's Lung Balm, Battle Ax Plug tobacco, Syrup of Figs, and Ayer's Hair Vigor, his message was: "Warning—The people of Genoa and vicinity are hereby warned against purchasing any articles from the Indian pupils without they show written permit from the superintendent properly signed and stamped."[8]

When Chauncey arrived to take the position of disciplinarian he had his work cut out for him. The Carlisle *Indian Helper* reported in December 1895 that "Chauncey Yellowrobe is occasionally heard from, in his work at the Genoa, Nebraska school. He says he is teaching the boys military tactics and enjoys his duties."[9] In what was probably a good career move considering the circumstances, he did not stay there long.

He did not seem pleased with his performance at Genoa or in the position itself. In a letter to Pratt written in 1897, he said, "I think that I have succeeded well with my work this year (at Fort Shaw) than I did last year (at Genoa)."[10] Chauncey is assumed to have been responsible for the introduction and cultivation of basketball at the school. Basketball was a sport largely introduced and taught by YMCA instructors. Fort Shaw had one of the first YMCA chapters at an Indian School, and Chauncey had been associated with "the Y" at Carlisle. The Fort Shaw women's basketball team went on to become basketball champions at the World's Fair in St. Louis in 1904. This team is the subject of the book *Full-Court Quest* written by Linda Peavy and Ursula Smith. Chauncey also coached the fledgling football team at the school.[11] It is easy to see how he could view his tenure at Shaw more productive that at Genoa. In that same letter he mentioned that Montana's rough roads limited his bicycle riding to the point that he had sold his "splendid bicycle … with rims (that) were made of solid paper."

9. The Indian Service School System

He was probably referring to a short-lived experiment that involved making bicycle tires out of pulp. "The tires are made of pulp produced from paper stock, and are of a sufficient durability to permit usage on carriage wheels as well as bicycles. It is claimed that the ties (sic) manufactured on the compartment plan are as easy riding as the most elastic pneumatics."[12]

10

On the Move

While being careful not to succumb to the "if it's not written down by a white man" syndrome, Chauncey's employment record during this time period seems confusing, incomplete, and often contradictory. While it may well be, as *The Indian Helper* says, that "since he left Carlisle he has occupied responsible positions as industrial teacher and disciplinarian at Sisseton, S. Dak., at Genoa, Nebr., and at Fort Shaw, Montana, having been promoted each transfer,"[1] nothing in his employment record would suggest it. The various publications from Carlisle were often intended to present the school and its graduates in the best possible way. Jacqueline Fear-Segal says that "articles and stories carried in the *Indian Helper* were slanted, sanitized, and clearly subjected to strict editorial control."[2] In Chauncey's case, early in his career, he frequently changed jobs; not all changes were promotions; there are discrepancies in title and salary; and his frank self-assessment after his first stay at Genoa indicates that he was far from satisfied. The next three or four years are even more uncertain, confusing, and disturbing—perhaps even more so than the image of Chauncey riding around Montana on a bicycle with paper tires.

After Chauncey's stints at Genoa and Fort Shaw, where he was and what he did in the Indian School Service are in question. Weinberg says that "In 1897, after a year spent at schools in Santee, Nebraska, and Fort Lewis, Colorado, he was appointed boys' disciplinarian at Fort Shaw School in Montana."[3] Perhaps she is referring to the Genoa School, and Chauncey himself lists the Santee Agency as his first job after Carlisle instead of Genoa. He does not list any position at Sisseton.

The Annual Report of the Commission of Indian Affairs never indicates that Chauncey taught at either Santee Boarding School or Fort Lewis, although *The Indian Helper* at Carlisle reported on August 26, 1898, that "Chauncey Yellowrobe, a graduate of the Indian School, who has been

10. On the Move

acting efficiently as assistant disciplinarian here for some time past, has secured a position as disciplinarian of the Indian School at Fort Lewis, Colorado, and leaves tonight for his new field of labor. He is a Sioux and a very fine example of the educated American Indian. -The Daily Herald, Aug. 24. Mr. Yellowrobe left yesterday morning, and carries with him the best wishes of a host of friends, all of whom can but respect and admire the indomitable pluck and perseverance which have ever dominated him from a youth when from the Indian camp he entered Carlisle, unable to speak English and was dressed in Indian attire, up to his present status of dignity, manliness and true business ability and power. Mr. Yellowrobe's Sioux tongue will not bend easily to some of our English twists and turns, but this is no drawback to him and is something which he will yet conquer by the same determined effort he has made to reach the point in language already attained."[4] Chauncey was welcomed to Carlisle in the *Indian Helper* on October 29, 1898. Perhaps owing to his friendship with Pratt, he served as Assistant Disciplinarian and apparently spent much of his brief tenure there visiting the students who were outing. As usual Chauncey made a good impression with the school/s white patrons. MRB from Yardley, Pennsylvania said, "Mr. Yellowrobe, your inspector, called a short time ago, and I found him most entertaining. You certainly did more to show your patrons and American citizens in general the possibilities in the Indian, by sending him out, than you could have possibly done in any other way. Always before, I had believed that the saying about the Indian returning to his blanket was quite true, but now I know, that instead, he can become an educated gentleman without even the suggestion of 'blanket!' I was very glad of the opportunity his call afforded me."[5]

It does not appear that he ever actually went to Fort Lewis, or at least that his employment there was ever documented, but in May of 1899 *The Indian Helper* printed that Chauncey Yellowrobe directs a change of address from Ft. Lewis Colorado to Rosebud Agency, South Dakota.[6] Weinberg says that he left Fort Lewis and returned to Rosebud as a result of "an adverse reaction to the altitude" there.[7] His next documented position was back at Fort Shaw as of June 30, 1900.

Weinberg also cites an *Indian Helper* article entitled "FT. SHAW TO THE FRONT" that reported, "We see by the Great Falls Tribune, Montana that a fine performance was given recently at the Grand Opera House, by the pupils of the Ft. Shaw Government School for the benefit of the soldiers' monument fund. It is said that there had never before been a more thoroughly pleased audience in the Opera House, and that the work of the students reflected great credit upon the school and its management. Chauncey Yellowrobe, a graduate of our school, ('95) appears to have made a hit. His remarks were earnest and forcibly delivered, says the Tribune, and the whole audience frequently applauded his expressions. He made a plea for non-reservation schools for the Indians. He eloquently urged that the Indians are anxious for communication with the whites and for citizenship, and modestly cited himself as an instance of what the non-reservation schools may accomplish. 'Five years ago I left Carlisle,' he said, 'and I am still on the warpath toward civilization.' The audience heartily approved his suggestions, having abundant evidence of what one non-reservation school had done."[8] There can be no doubt that the topic of the speech was certainly something Chauncey had talked about in the past, for example at the Congress of Nations, but the article is dated July 6, 1899. According to the Commissioner's report, he was not employed at Fort Shaw that time.[9] Even Weinberg says that "in 1900 he returned to Fort Shaw, Montana."[10] It was not until June of 1900 that he was actually reported as being employed at Fort Shaw as disciplinarian[11] It is not clear what he did or where he did it between August 1898 and the beginning of the 1900 school year. Apparently, he spent the summer of 1899 in Rosebud recuperating, but he is not listed as an employee of the Indian Bureau or the Indian School Service there or anywhere during the rest of that year. During 1901, Yellow Robe is listed as an industrial teacher at Fort Berthold in Montana with an annual salary of $660—down from the $720 he was making at Fort Shaw.[12] This assignment is not mentioned in Weinberg's book. The next year, he is listed as a teacher back at Genoa making $800 as the disciplinarian.[13]

Scott Riney says that Chauncey Yellow Robe began working at Rapid City Indian School in 1904 or 1905.[14] This seems like a logical deduction made by counting back from a letter written in 1913 by Jesse F. House, the superintendent of the Rapid City school saying that he had been employed there for "about nine years."[15] The problem with that estimate is that he is not shown as an employee at Rapid City for either year. The earliest he could have been employed there is in 1906—leaving three years totally unaccounted for.

One published exchange with Carlisle (now the *Red Man and Helper* newspaper) was in a letter written to Pratt and printed in part on Christmas, 1903. "An excellent letter from Chauncey Yellowrobe, '95, now at

10. On the Move

Chauncey Yellow Robe and Lillian Springer were married at the Harney Hotel in Rapid City, South Dakota, on May 22, 1906 (courtesy Minnilusa Historical Association).

Rosebud, South Dakota, shows up the Indian situation in no uncertain terms. He is fearful that the Indians are to be exterminated through whiskey. The way the law protects the Indian on the reservation border is something like this: If an Indian goes off the reservation and buys whiskey from a white man and then sells it to his tribal brother he is breaking the United States law but not so with the white man who sold it to the Indian. Whiskey is one of the greatest evils on the reservation today, our correspondent thinks."[16]

Yellow Robe's other correspondence with General Pratt all appear to have been written from Rosebud during the 1903–1904 time period. The only clue to what might have been going on during this time period is found in a report Chauncey submitted to the Indian School Service (Report 5-351) in 1919. In that report he responded to the statement," if you have ever separated from the Service give reasons briefly," he stated "on account of ill health."[17] What is not clear is whether he was referring to the "lost years" or the altitude problem when he was reportedly assigned to Fort Lewis. As mentioned previously, it was a common practice at Carlisle to embellish the accomplishments of its graduates for the benefit of the institution, and previous biographers have not addressed these issues. Even accepting a measure of bureaucratic inaccuracy, questions about the inconsistencies remain.

11

The Rapid City Indian School

When Chauncey went to work at the Rapid City Indian School, whether in 1904, 1905, or 1906 as an industrial arts teacher, he began what would be his longest and last assignment with the Indian School System. He would also meet his future wife, Lillian Springer, who was a nurse at the school. The superintendent during most of that time was Jesse F. House, but Yellow Robe also worked with S.A.M. Young and Sharon R. Mote. In *The Rapid City Indian School, 1898–1933*, Scott Riney says that "none of the superintendents, however, not even Superintendent House, were as emblematic of the school's mission and its place in Indian lives as Lakota disciplinarian Chauncey Yellow Robe."[1] So important was Yellow Robe to the school that some sources refer to him as the head of the school. It was during this time of his life that Chauncey became more outspoken and active in Indian advocacy. While it can be asserted that his tenure at the Rapid City School was successful by some standards, it is also very clear that his outside interests and later the responsibilities of being a single parent diverted both his time and attention away from his job.

In 1913, Superintendent House recommended that Chauncey (referred to as C.Y. Robe) be made disciplinarian at the school. In a letter to the Commissioner of Indian Affairs he said,

> The Industrial Teacher, Mr. C.Y. Robe, is a graduate of the Carlisle Indian School and has had considerable experience as a Disciplinarian. He has been employed here about nine years and is a very trustworthy man and I believe he would prove fairly satisfactory as a disciplinarian.
>
> The only thing which is not quite in accordance with my ideas is that he is married and has a family and consequently would not be staying in the boys' building at night. He is now acting disciplinarian and has filled the position temporarily at other times.[2]

Chauncey Yellow Robe

An original building at the Rapid City Indian School. Although his work took him to different places in the Indian School System, the majority of Chauncey Yellow Robe's professional life was spent at the Rapid City Indian School (courtesy South Dakota State Historical Society, South Dakota Digital Archives, 2007-12-11-019).

While "fairly satisfactory" might not be considered as a ringing endorsement or vote of confidence, the transfer was approved. John Mote, the son of Sharon A. Mote who was superintendent during the last few years of Chauncey's tenure at the school, said that "Yellow Robe's title was changed from Disciplinarian to Boy's Adviser. Dad felt that strict discipline was important at the school, and was sometimes upset when he felt that Yellow Robe was failing to maintain such discipline."[3] The issues of Chauncey's living arrangement, job performance, and propensity to come and go from the school did not go away until he resigned.

On October 23, 1923, Superintendent S.A.M. Young directed Chauncey and Mrs. Walters, the school matron, to "take steps to put a

11. The Rapid City Indian School

stop to the practice" of students who were jumping on the running boards of cars to hitch rides.[4] There was little doubt that the boundaries of the school were not particularly secure, and other than to tell them to stop, it is not clear what Yellow Robe and Walters could do. The school had been rocked by a tragedy in 1910 when two runaway male students from Pine Ridge were killed by a train.[5]

Superintendent Mote's letters and reprimands started soon after his assignment to Rapid City. He clearly felt that stricter discipline needed to be established among the students and employees. Whether he micromanaged or simply saw more than previous superintendents might be open to interpretation, but he was not reluctant to deal with issues he saw as he moved around the campus and town. As chief disciplinarian, many of these ended up with Chauncey.

In mid–December of 1925, he happened upon boys playing basketball with employees in the gymnasium around 7:00 p.m. He was concerned about that for a couple of reasons. First, it was during the time the boys were supposed to be receiving religious instruction. Second, he saw that students were present during the employees' physical education hour. It was not suggested that Chauncey was present; only that he needed to be more conscientious about the whereabouts of the boys.[6] Another related incident took place on January 5, 1927, when Mote wrote Chauncey about two boys who were in the gym at the wrong time. One of the boys, Clarence Raymond, had said that they had been dismissed and allowed to go to the gym by Chauncey.[7]

In February of 1926, Mote wrote to Chauncey and the school matron, Mrs. Walters that his inspection of the toilets on both the large and small boys' side found them "not as clean as they ought to be." He indicated that they needed to be "perfectly white and clean … all the way down to the floor."[8] Mote was clearly "surprised and disappointed" that Chauncey did not attend the first employees' meeting of the 1927 school year. Both the disciplinarian and school matron were absent prompting Mote to comment that it was unfortunate that people who held these important positions took their responsibilities so lightly.[9]

This incident came on the heels of another occasion in July when Chauncey seemed to have been absent without permission. Yellow Robe had been elected a delegate to the state convention of the Isaac Walton League in Deadwood. He was an avid fisherman. Rather than ask permission or talk to Mote personally, Chauncey left a hurriedly written note with Dallas DeCory—another school employee. He asked Dallas to give it to Mote and to serve as his stand-in at the boys' dormitory in his absence. Not surprisingly, Mote was not pleased. In fact, it appears that his anger seems to bleed through his words and syntax. He wrote

> I cannot understand how you can be taking your work seriously and (how) the disciplinary situation reached the tangled mess that it has been in the last few days and on top of it all you leave without permission to be gone a day or more. A little over a week ago while Mr. Day (George A. Day, senior clerk) was in charge you left the school and nobody seemed to know where you had gone and when you would be back. You were gone for three days and you did not even sign a request for the three days you were gone until sent for and asked to sign, neither have you signed any request for today's leave of absence.
>
> I am seriously considering putting the matter up to the Office that the disciplinary situation at this school is not satisfactory. You have not seemed to have a proper grip on the situation. You go to town whenever you feel like it without notifying the office and I have frequently sent work to you and found you gone....
>
> I want you to see me immediately upon your return and let us come to a full understanding of your responsibility.[10]

Perhaps not so coincidentally, shortly thereafter James H. McGregor, the district superintendent, wrote Mote questioning the wisdom of Chauncey's not living in the boys' dormitory. He acknowledged Chauncey's years of service, but concluded by stating that "I do not know about Mr. Yellowrobe's family condition, nor how inconvenient it would be to make the change suggested, but I do believe, however, that it would be much safer to have the disciplinarian in the building." It appears that the letter was forwarded by Mote to Chauncey. Even more interestingly, there is a handwritten note on the letter (appearing to be in someone other than Chauncey's handwriting) that simply states "Can't move me."[11]

Mote's response to McGregor's letter contained the question, "Would you advise that he be required to live in the dormitory or be replaced by another disciplinarian?"[12] When the question and situation reached the Assistant Commissioner of Indian Affairs E.B. Merill, he responded by saying to Mote that "this Office knows of no reason why you should not instruct Mr. Yellow Robe to room with the boys. This is an administrative question and you should use your own discretion in the matter. However, it should be understood that you will be held responsible for results."[13] McGregor had been fairly blunt with Mote in his letter:

> coming down to cold-blooded facts, shall a hundred boys be deprived of the influence and protection that would be afforded them by having their

11. The Rapid City Indian School

disciplinarian in the building with them where they can consult him on subjects of morals, health, discipline, etc.? As I see it, the welfare of these hundred boys, that I will term as fatherless, are jeopardized in order that Mr. Yellow Robe may protect his two motherless girls. At the same time, the Government is paying a man to be a father, in the fullest sense, to these large boys who need and deserve and are entitled to this special fatherly contact that Mr. Yellow Robe is so well qualified to give. I appreciate the fact that he has recently sprung into prominence as a possible candidate for Congress, and that his participation in the President's entertainment has given him a standing that he did not have previously. This fact, however, should not make him less amenable to our regulations and policies but rather more anxious to fall in line.[14]

Mote responded that he had shown the letter to Yellow Robe and had a "heart to heart" talk with him. According to Mote, Chauncey had said that he would probably be making arrangements to have his daughter cared for elsewhere and could live in the dormitory.[15]

During the interim between the letter from McGregor and Mote's reply, the letters of reprimand came quickly and often. Mote was clearly in the documentation phase of whatever was going to happen, and Chauncey was making plans as well.

In fairness to Chauncey, it should be noted that most of the reprimands and concerns came in the last two or three years of his service and most came from Superintendent Mote. While his personnel record did include warnings and reprimands it should also be noted that he was called upon for input, advice, and even to represent "Indians" at a ceremony involving the President of the United States.

One such occasion took place in 1917 when Chauncey was asked to go to the Sisseton Indian Agency to recruit students. Chauncey wrote a letter to Superintendent House indicating that he had arrived. It was dated August 4, 1917, but obviously he meant to write September 4 since the Indian Fair he had been sent to attend and work took place from September 3 to 5. A few days later Chauncey wrote to House saying that "this is my sixth day on the reservation and haven't got a student yet."[16] He even expanded his search to a nearby church conference but was unsuccessful there too. He did report that he found one boy who wanted to go to Rapid City, but he was twenty-five years old and in the fourth grade. Another young man, a former student at Rapid City, was a possibility until he found out that he had been drafted. House told Chauncey that unless he had specific leads he should return to the school.

Chauncey was frequently dispatched to nearby reservations to bring back runaway or truant students. These forays were often tense and even threatening, since parents and relatives of students frequently either encouraged them to run away or harbored them while they were on the loose. Being Lakota, Chauncey was an effective representative of the school. He made such trips to the Rosebud, Sisseton, Pine Ridge, and Cheyenne River reservations. He was of great value when it was necessary to bridge cultures or to interact with the white residents of Rapid City. Superintendent House sent Yellow Robe and two other Indians to the bars and saloons of Rapid City to make undercover buys of whiskey. While the presence of alcohol at the school was always a matter of concern, this particular covert operation seemed to be directed more at the "considerable drunkenness of the part of Indians" in general around Rapid City.[17]

Just like when he was at Carlisle, Chauncey was clearly a good person to have around. He was obviously respected by the students and community in general. Even those who became critical of his job performance acknowledged that he carried himself with dignity. Superintendent Mote's son commented that "I always had the impression that my parents had a high regard for Yellow Robe."[18]

Another occasion when the school was glad to have Chauncey associated with it occurred on August 4, 1927, when one of the biggest things ever to happen in South Dakota took place. President Calvin Coolidge and his wife were enjoying an extended vacation in the Black Hills that summer. They were staying at the Game Lodge in Custer State Park. Although the trip and Coolidge's role in the celebration would soon become lost as a result of his surprising the world with the brief announcement, handed out to reporters on pieces of paper he cut himself, that he did not "choose to run for President in Nineteen twenty-eight."[19] Silent Cal seemed to enjoy jerking the reporters around from his temporary office at the Rapid City High School as much as he was enjoying his vacation. He attended the "Days of '76" celebration in Deadwood where Chauncey, accompanied by his oldest daughter, Rosebud, made him an honorary chief. The newspaper proclaimed that over three hundred Sioux in full "war paint" were present as Chauncey, Rosebud, and Standing Bear coronated Coolidge as "Chief Leading Eagle."

A June 23, 2015, article In *Indian Country Today* quoted a June 23, 1927, article in the *Sioux Country Pioneer* that said that Chauncey himself "suggested (that) he (Coolidge) be adopted into the tribe."[20] This was no small event for several reasons. It was reported that Coolidge considered

11. The Rapid City Indian School

At the "chiefing" ceremony of President Calvin Coolidge as Chief Leading Eagle on August 4, 1927. To the president's left: Chauncey Yellow Robe; Rosebud, his oldest daughter; and Standing Bear.

himself to be a great friend to America's Indians tribes. On many occasions he commented on the extreme poverty he saw on the Indian reservations. In 1924, Coolidge signed the Indians Citizen Act which granted citizenship for all members of America's Indian tribes. Unfortunately, public policy changed very little despite his concerns.

The event also produced what has come to be regarded as one of the most interesting, if not ridiculous pictures of any American President ever. There is no doubt that the Indians were sincere in their efforts. The headdress alone was valued at more than $2500 and contained both golden and bald eagle feathers. Craftsman and collector Robert F. Backus provided the feathers and buckskin used in the ceremony. The sincerity of the Indians, and Chauncey in particular, can clearly be seen in the photographs taken there and in his comments. After first speaking in Lakota, Chauncey

Chauncey Yellow Robe

said in English, "I congratulate you in the name of the Sioux Nation, and express the hope that you will continue to guide the will of this Nation to its great destiny."[21] It is not clear how or when Chauncey had been given the authority to speak for the entire Sioux Nation, but he clearly seized the opportunity. An article in the *Sioux County Pioneer* went so far as to say that the original idea to "adopt" Coolidge was Chauncey's.[22]

For the Indians, and especially for Chauncey, this event was certainly not just "entertainment" for the President. In retrospect, Chauncey and the others came very close to being "show Indians." Chauncey's motives might have been self-serving. He might have been thinking about his fledgling political career. Clearly, the person who benefited most from the new coverage was Rosebud. Chauncey insisted that she be part of the ceremony. The grace and beauty of this University of South Dakota student captured the hearts and imaginations of people around the nation. Chief Leading Eagle was resplendent and dignified in his headdress, but Coolidge's embarrassment or awkwardness was evident. He apparently felt much more comfortable in his cowboy attire—chaps, boots, and ten-gallon hat—and was seen frequently dressed that way while in South Dakota.

12

Lillian

One of the main attractions at the Harney Hotel in Rapid City was an aquarium in the café that was home to several large trout. Customers could drop a hookless fly into the water to see a "rise." One of the larger fish was reportedly so tame that it would allow patrons to rub its sides and belly. But on May 22, 1906, it was not the trout that gained the attention of guests and passersby. It was the attractive couple and their small group of friends who were assembled there. The wedding of Chauncey Yellow Robe and Lillian Belle Springer was not like most held in Rapid City, South Dakota, at that time. He was a dark skinned "Sioux," and she was a fair-skinned, blonde German. Theirs was an atypical interracial marriage—one that was likely to get a rise out of some people and one that was still illegal in several states.

The Harney Hotel was built was built in 1885–86 by John Brennan. Brennan was one of the founders of Rapid City. The Harney was considered the town's best hotel for many years—well into the twentieth century. Although their wedding did not take place in a church, the officiant was the minister–Reverend Mr. W.H. Sparling. He was also the minister who officiated at the marriage of Carrie Ingalls, sister of Laura Ingalls Wilder, to David Swanzey in 1912. The superintendent of the Rapid City Indian School, Jesse House, "gave the bride away." Neither Chauncey nor Lillie had any family members attend, but several friends and colleagues were present. After the wedding, they honeymooned at nearby Hot Springs, Deadwood, and Sylvan Lake in what is now Custer State Park.

Lillian Belle Springer was the daughter of Henry Springer and Emma Scholer Springer. She was born in Crookston, Minnesota in 1885. Her paternal grandparents, Johan Jacob Springer and Katrina Gisler Springer had emigrated from Neftenbach, Switzerland, in 1854. Her maternal grandparents, Andreas Scholar and Maria Barbara Hurst Scholar, lived in

Chauncey Yellow Robe

Voegisheim, Loerrach, Baden, Germany. When Lillian was three years old her family moved to Tacoma, Washington. She attended school there until she enrolled in the Maria Beard Deaconess Hospital Nurses' Training School in Spokane, Washington—incorrectly identified in Weinberg's book as Maria Bilard Hospital.[1,2]

The hospital was opened in 1896 and soon added the nursing school. The Deaconess Movement was an outgrowth of Methodist women's mission work, and several deaconesses at this particular hospital were native Germans. The movement originated on the East Coast in the 1880s as a way of ministering to the spiritual and physical needs of the sick and needy. The training was rigorous and demanding. The doctors at the hospital taught the classes. The nursing students lived on the site and worked six days a week on twelve-hour shifts. If the workload permitted they were given four hours off on Sundays.

Lillian Springer joined Jessie Scott, Lillian Spencer, and Audrey Weymire in graduating in 1902 as the school's second graduating class.[3] She began working with a local doctor. Lillian (Lillie) took the civil service exam in nursing "for fun to see if I could pass,"[4] and apparently because she felt stifled in her private work. In July of 1905, she was offered a position at the Rapid City Indian School. She left Tacoma in August of that same year. Her contract was for one year, and she confided in friends that she would probably be returning to Washington after that year—she did not.

In *Taking Assimilation to Heart*, Katherine Ellinghaus says that "marriages between white women and indigenous men were rare occurrences."[5] Rare perhaps in the general population, but common among educated Native American men. Men like the ones with whom Chauncey had come to associate in the Society of American Indians. Both Carlos Montezuma and Charles Eastman were married to white women. Montezuma married Marie Keller who was born in Romania. Eastman married Elaine Goodale whose parents were both from prominent New England families. Richard Pratt affirmed his support of marriages between Indians and whites in a letter to Montezuma. "I spoke to the Presbyterian preachers in San Francisco the day before yesterday. After I was through one of them asked me if I believed in intermarriage. I, of course affirmed my position and instanced not only a number of happy and distinguished intermarriages (which will present themselves to you), but the grand result from the progeny of such Indian marriages."[6] It is not surprising that these men who

12. Lillian

lived, and were models of, assimilated lives would marry white women. Neither is it surprising that such marriages often generated discussion, controversy, and tension.

That did not seem to be the case for the (Yellow) Robes. Surprisingly for the place and time, Lillie and Chauncey seem to have not been bothered by much overt prejudice or discrimination. He frequently commented about how well he was received by her family and friends in Tacoma. Weinberg quotes from a letter written by Lillie to her friend Clara:

> So, you are surprised because I married into a different race and you think it awful. But it is not—in years to come people will not think it so. Mr. Robe is more than my equal in every way. I am proud to own his name—he is of a good family & I am, so why shouldn't our offspring be bright, intelligent and healthy. I do not see why you feel sorry—I do not. The folks (her parents) are perfectly satisfied and look at it the way I do. Since we have been married, we have made a great many friends—people here admire Mr. Robe greatly—he is respected anywhere as much as anyone.[7]

The only reported incident involving them as a couple took place in Denver while they were attending a Society of American Indian conference. According to Weinberg, Chauncey told his daughter Rosebud about overhearing disparaging remarks made about an Indian man and white women in the hotel bar. They quickly retreated to their room and stacked the furniture against the door for the rest of the night. Lilly proved to be extremely prophetic in her assessment of their "offspring." The Yellow Robes had three daughters—Rosebud, Chaucina, and Evelyn. All three were extraordinary women in their respective ways. Much more will be said about them later.

Lillian Springer Yellow Robe was forty-two years old when she died. According to a great-granddaughter, she suffered from throat cancer and spent much of the time during the last few years of her life in a wheelchair or bed. Her death certificate starkly attributes her death to starvation.[8]

Rosebud, the oldest daughter was born in 1907; Chaucina was born in 1908 (or 1909, 1910, or 1914); and the youngest child, Evelyn, was born in 1920. Lillie's grace and temperament were revealed in an interesting and innocently charming anecdote told by John A. Mote, the son of the superintendent at Rapid City.

> When I was about seven, I developed a friendship with one of her daughters and used to visit her in her home. During one visit I persuaded the daughter to go into a closet with me where we would take off our clothes. We hadn't been

Chauncey Yellow Robe

in the closet long before her mother started calling for us. When she discovered us, her response to our partially-clad appearance was gentle. As she buttoned up my shirt, she told us that what we had been doing wasn't a good idea. I was scared to death that she would tell my parents about this incident and was so grateful that she never did.[9]

Although the gentlemanly Mote did not identify which Yellow Robe daughter was involved, it would seem that Evelyn (born the same year as Mote) was the likely co-perpetrator. Mote became a minister in the United Methodist Church in the Baltimore and Washington, D.C., areas for 59 years before retiring. He was widely recognized and respected as a humanitarian and civil rights activist. He was responsible for integrating Brookland United Methodist Church in Washington, D.C., where African Americans had previously been told they were not welcome. Evelyn Yellow Robe Finkbeiner graduated from and taught at Mount Holyoke College. She became a world-renowned speech pathologist. She died in 2016. Apparently no one was traumatized or emotionally thwarted by a little playing doctor in the closet.

13

Relationship to Sitting Bull

As Chauncey's reputation grew, so did questions about aspects of his background and lineage. He said in "My Boyhood Days" that his father was "a son of a hereditary chief. He equally won his title of chieftainship as a fearless warrior, runner, and great hunter."[1] His daughter, Rosebud, echoed that statement almost verbatim in her book *Toneweya and the Eagles:* "My grandfather was named Tasinagi, or Yellow Robe. He was son of a hereditary chief. He had won his title to chieftainship as a fearless warrior and great hunter."[2] Both were no doubt trying to show that Chauncey was descended from a long line of chiefs and leaders on his father's side.

While not complicating the matter for white readers, it could be pointed out that American Indians did not use the term chief at all, and that it was a white invention intended to make it easier to deal with one designated individual rather than the complicated and fluid governing structures of the Indians. Titles like hereditary "chieftainship" and "Indian princess" suggest a royalty among the Indians that most would say really did not seem to have existed at all. Luther Standing Bear said that "there were no social strata so definite that some (positions of leadership) were unattainable by reason of class or birth, but there were individuals and groups who were recognized by virtue of superior intelligence and capacity.... In many and various ways there were individuals who stood out from the rest."[3]

This confusion was at one time expressed by Rosebud Yellow Robe's husband Alfred Frantz who said in a letter to his granddaughter, "He (Chauncey) was the seventh in a line of hereditary chiefs (usually men became chiefs because of outstanding achievements); I myself did not know about hereditary ones until I married your grandmother (Chauncey's daughter Rosebud)."[4] Although the hereditary chiefdom did seem to exist among the Sisseton and Wahpeton,[5] it is highly likely that Tasinagi was a member of a governing council (as opposed to being a chief) and that membership on that council could, in fact, "be handed down from father to son, but the governing council had the right to approve." In *Oglala Religion*, William Powers goes on to add that most "modern Oglalas still assert that chieftainship was hereditary."[6]

Why Chauncey and Rosebud were not content with a "chieftainship," not a very Indian sounding title at all, based solely on merit is unclear, but the title hereditary chief came to be applied to Chauncey as well. It is clear that the family, both in terms of the father's and mother's supposed linage, was both known and distinguished. Tasinagi was a signatory of the Fort Laramie Treaty of 1868 but simply did not have the status and notoriety of Iron Shell, Spotted Tale and others. Nonetheless, he was noteworthy in his own right.

Chauncey seems to have experienced a little of the "if a white man doesn't write it down it didn't happen" problem himself when it came to his knowledge about Sitting Bull and especially his mother's relationship to him. On December 8, 1908, Chauncey wrote a letter to Doane Robinson, the State Historian and Secretary of the South Dakota Historical Society. Chauncey questioned comments Robinson had made during a speech that was made before the Academy of Science and Letters and quoted in the *Sioux City Tribune*. Robinson had "declared that Sitting Bull was a Medicine Man and not a chief." Chauncey said that "I wish to take this liberty in saying that Sitting Bull was always Chief of his people (the Sioux Nation) and not a medicine man as you have stated. He was simply a great general in his time and the true history of him has never been recorded. Some of my relatives are now living who were close associates of Sitting Bull."[7]

Robinson responded immediately and definitively that Chauncey was "not quite correctly informed in relation to Sitting Bull. He was unquestionably the leading spirit among the Sioux in the time of their heroic fight for their lands, culminating in the campaign of 1876, but he was not in the ordinary sense a military man at all. It was his boast as long as he lived that he had never killed. While he was one of the chief advisors in the movement at Little Big Horn and thruout [sic] the campaign, he did not take part in the battle at all, but was in a medicine tepee, upon the high ground between the Little Horn and the Big Horn." Robinson concluded

13. Relationship to Sitting Bull

that "he was a medicine man and not a general or military man at all."[8] It is interesting that in his letter Chauncey said that some of his relatives were "close associates" of Sitting Bull, but he stopped short of saying that his mother was a niece.

Robinson's letter must have had some impact on Chauncey's opinion because some years later in 1926 and 1927, an article that was carried by most major newspapers reported that Chauncey, "an educated full-blooded Sioux,"[9] had repeatedly emphasized that Sitting Bull was a spiritual leader, not a military one, and had certainly not killed Custer himself, nor had he had any hand in the Battle of The Little Big Horn at all. In those articles Chauncey was once again identified as a nephew of Sitting Bull, and those stories might have given impetus to a closer examination of that relationship.

On October 19, 1928, Sharon Mote, superintendent of the Rapid City Indian School where Chauncey worked, received a letter from the chief clerk of the Office of Indian Affairs saying that the library in the office had received an inquiry as to the "relationship between Chauncy [sic] Yellow Robe and Sitting Bull."[10] Mote was directed to respond to the inquiry. On October 23, 1928, Mote wrote a letter to Chauncey, who at that time was filming *The Silent Enemy* in Canada, directing him to send a letter explaining the details of that relationship to Commissioner of Indian Affairs and that he (Mote) be sent a copy. Mote asked, "Was your mother's father a brother of Sitting Bull? Or just which one of your immediate parents or grandparents was a brother or sister of Sitting Bull?"[11] On that same day, Mote wrote the Commissioner a letter in which he said that "I regret to advise that we have nothing in our records to indicate this relationship."[12]

Unfortunately, there is no record of Chauncey's reply. Although he did write Mote several times after that, the relationship to Sitting Bull was not mentioned. It is not clear from whom that initial inquiry came. Likewise, it is not clear if the writer was trying to discredit Yellow Robe or to authenticate his claims. Shortly after Sitting Bull was killed, there were conflicting claims about his true descendants. Later there was disagreement between "relatives" about the return of the few possessions of his that were kept and still later there was the issue of the location of his reburial. No other official correspondence about the subject exists, but once again, much later, Rosebud's husband further clouded the issue by writing that "there is also the relation to Sitting Bull, which is not clear to me. Rosebud has a different story practically every time. I think she is a grand niece, but won't swear."[13] One of the present-day Yellow Robes has said that she had always been told that two of Yellow Robe's (Tasinagi) several wives were sisters and both were nieces of Sitting Bull. There was much division among the Standing Rock Sioux about Sitting Bull's character and reputation almost immediately after his death, and that continued for many years.

Different people claim to possess sworn affidavits that the Yellow Robes were lineal relatives of Sitting Bull, and reportedly one of Rosebud's prized possessions was one of his saddle blankets. No written evidence exists of any of Sitting Bull's property being retained except for a lock of his hair and leggings he was wearing when he was killed. Perhaps kinship to Sitting Bull was a matter of convenience rather than fact. Even the tragic Lost Bird of Wounded Knee, or Zintkala Nuni, fostered the rumor that she was Sitting Bull's daughter as her personal life collapsed and her professional life in movies and wild west shows waned.

Chauncey also claimed kinship with Iron Plume, whom he referred to as uncle. Iron Plume himself is the subject of some confusion and misunderstanding. He is sometimes erroneously referred to as American Horse—a name which seems to have been fairly commonly given and taken at the time. Chauncey's uncle was the warrior leader killed at the Battle of Slim Buttes.

14

The Society of American Indians

Like many other Native Americans who were articulate and educated, Chauncey Yellow Robe became involved with the Society of American Indians during the first part of the 20th century. Rosebud Yellow Robe wrote that "my father became very well known for his activities, first with The Society of American Indians. He was much sought after by many organizations as a speaker and soon became known as a 'bridge between two cultures.'"[1] Marjorie Weinberg further addressed his participation in the SAI by saying that "nationally, Chauncey was active in the Society of American Indians, an organization of educated Native Americans devoted to progress and acculturation."[2]

The organization itself was the first national effort in pan–Indianism— an endeavor made extremely problematic as a result of years of tribal warfare and competition. Sociology professor Fayette Avery McKenzie of Ohio State University and a number of representative, educated American Indians met on April 3 and 4, 1911, at Ohio State University in Columbus to lay the groundwork for the SAI. The Indians present were Dr. Charles A. Eastman (Santee Sioux), Dr. Carlos Montezuma (Yavapai Apache), Thomas L. Sloan (Omaha), Hon. Chas. E. Dagenett (*Peoria*), Miss Laura M. Cornelius (*Oneida*) and Henry Standing Bear (*Oglala Lakota*). While they were there the University President W.O. Thompson and Columbus city leaders invited them to hold their first annual conference on the Ohio State campus. They adopted the temporary name of the American Indian Association and sent out over 4000 invitations. This call to individual Indians, not tribal representatives, and progressive, supportive whites, who were permitted to join as associate members, resulted in a national conference that took place over the Columbus Day weekend, October 12–17, 1911.

Chauncey Yellow Robe

Several things about the SAI were apparent from the beginning. Its Indian leaders were committed to the idea of assimilation both in a general sense, and in their own personal lives. It was clear that William Pratt was their ideological hero. They were educated and Christianized. They also felt that, being the educated representatives of their race, they had both the right and the responsibility to speak and advocate for Native Americans at the national level. The SAI proved to leave a literate and reflective legacy. It published the *Quarterly Journal of the American Indian* (1913–1915), which was renamed *American Indian Magazine* (1916–1920).

It would be a considerable stretch to say that he was one of the organization's leaders, but the fact that Chauncey Yellow Robe was involved in any way with the Society of American Indians is somewhat surprising. The fact that he was a frequent contributor to its publications, spoke at several conferences, and was on the Board of Advisors could be considered a testimony to his eloquence and charisma. The SAI was comprised of "educated Indians" and was considered by many, including some of its own members, as elitist. Chauncey did not have the educational credentials or work history of people like Charles Eastman, Carlos Montezuma, or Henry Roe Cloud. It was remarkable that his name frequently was included in the same sentence as these men. His education had gone no further than Carlisle, which was viewed at best as a grammar school and at worst like little more than a vocational school. His work history had been undistinguished and had been exclusively in Indian Service boarding schools as a teacher or as a disciplinarian. His moments in the sun had been while he was at Carlisle—first as an interpreter in Washington and then as a docent at the Chicago World's Fair. Therein probably lies the reason for his inclusion in the SAI—like Montezuma, he was a favorite of Pratt, and Pratt was held in very high esteem by the SAI.

One of the most divisive of a host of internal controversies in the SAI was whether or not Indian Bureau employees could represent Indian interests instead of government interests. In a letter urging SAI members to attend the organization's third annual conference, the Secretary—Treasurer, Arthur C. Parker felt it necessary to say that "some rumors have been circulated that we are controlled by the 'government' and that we have contracted to go to Denver in 1915 to attend a 'wild west show.'" Both statements are absolutely untrue."[3] Chauncey privately took a definite position about most SAI issues and shared it with friends and confidants like Dr. Montezuma and Richard Pratt. He seems to have seen himself as being

14. The Society of American Indians

personally involved and in the fray with the political machinations rampant in the Society. In what appears to be a hurriedly written, disjointed letter to Montezuma on May 6, 1912. Yellow Robe (writing from Cut Meat, South Dakota, on the Rosebud Reservation) lamented, "I am still in the fight but about to be killed. They had Dagnett (Dagenett) man elected President of our Society (SAI)." He continued, seeming to suggest that it might be better to try to "start over" with better, more representative leadership that was not controlled by the Indian Bureau.

> If anybody sinks me, I generally take some one [sic] along and I will not give up following my enemies. Miss Cornelius and Dr. Eastman are not favorable to the leaders high of certain ones you understand. You and those two leaving the society and your words against its officers will mean complete death. You three could continue or you alone can continue and you will surprise to see the qualities of young Indian men that awaits to follow you. We can draft a constitution with few good members and that will get the good opinion of the best people. Do you care?
>
> Many of us rather follow you. A man having a great reputation. Dr. Eastman, Miss Cornelius and you can easily command the interest and serious thoughts of the best people among the whites. Quite a number of us thought of this—to draw up a constitution and pass around to the picked best Indians that we know will mean honest and who are ready to fall in line with us and with officers in Chicago. We can quietly start in our work. You better write me soon. Many of us are waiting. It will only waste my time to keep after these fellows (who) do not mean honest interest. They cunningly try to single me out and put me down.[4]

Yellow Robe was apparently respected enough and prolific enough to have several articles published in the Society's *Quarterly Journal of the American Indian* and *American Indian Magazine*. Impressively, one was a personal biography ("My Boyhood Days") that described his boyhood days up until the time he met Pratt and attended Carlisle. Published in that same edition was Montezuma's "Let My People Go," which received much more attention, acclaim, and criticism.

His deeply held conviction about the inherently abusive, personal and cultural, treatment of Indians in the wild west shows was one topic in his speeches and articles that seemed to resonate with other members of the Society. Although he never mentioned it, his first-hand experiences with "the demented Indian" incident in Atlanta and the fact that his brother, Joseph, had been a member of the Buffalo Bill show that toured Europe in 1906 certainly had an impact on him.[5] In speeches at the SAI's third annual conference in Denver in 1913, and at the fourth annual

Chauncey Yellow Robe

conference in Madison, Wisconsin, the next year, Yellow Robe talked about the "evil and degrading influence of commercializing the Indian before the world," and he said that "the commercialization of Indians was "the greatest hindrance, injustice, and detriment to the present progress of American Indians toward civilization."[6] These speeches were printed in the *Quarterly Journal* and probably reached far more people that way than through the paltry numbers who attended the conferences, where it frequently seemed like everyone present was also a presenter. In fact, Chauncey revealed in a letter to Carlos Montezuma that although he was invited to speak at the conference in Denver and was given the freedom to select his own topic, when he got there he discovered that he was not included on the program.[7] He was allowed to make a short speech as appeasement. In 1917, when the magazine printed a "special Sioux number," or edition, Chauncey was asked and contributed an article entitled "The Fighting Sioux," which was largely an argument for why Native Americans should and would volunteer to fight in World War I.[8] However, this article did not receive the attention or acclaim that ones by Arthur Parker ("The Sioux Outbreak of 1862") and Charles Eastman ("The Sioux of Yesterday and Today") attained. In that same issue, the editor identified "able business men who were born in tepees. Some of these younger men who are succeeding are Chauncey Yellow Robe of Rapid City, Henry and Luther Standing Bear of Pine Ridge.... A survey of Sioux achievement even as brief as this proves the capacity of the Sioux mind and the ability of the Sioux to take on 'civilization' and work with and for it."[9] Yellow Robe served on the largely insignificant Advisory Board in 1917, 1919, and 1921. By that time, the SAI was essentially fractured and fragmented beyond repair. The only other advisory board member of note during that time was Henry Standing Bear.

Like many other prominent Native American leaders of the time, Chauncey was a Freemason. There are many interesting and somewhat fanciful explanations about the Indians' apparent affinity to Freemasonry. Some suggest that a form of Freemasonry existed in the Americas among the Indians long before white contact. Denslow charitably calls these "absurd myths."[10] Parallels have been drawn between Native American secret societies and Masonry. Both certainly do seem to have sacred symbols, greetings, and words. Rather than investigate obscure similarities, symbols, and legends, it again appears that the best explanation is the simplest one. In *Native American Freemasonry*, Joy Porter thoughtfully

14. The Society of American Indians

opines that "the larger truth is that the majority of things that attracted Indian Masons to the fraternity were the same things that attracted any man. For example, Masonry offered to extend kinship relationships; within a guiding organizational metaphor of the family ('mother' lodges, 'sister' lodges, etc.) the fraternity made 'brothers' out of strangers. This would have attracted any number of non–WASP communities, Indians included."[11]

Many of the leaders of the Society of American Indians and other leading native scholars were Masons. One such person was Dr. Arthur C. Parker. Parker, a Seneca, said that "Masons and Masonic support have done many valuable things for the Indian race, and the part of Masonry in the civilization of the red man is no small one, though it is largely unrecorded, for Masons do not flaunt their charities. It would not be an overstatement, however, to say that Masonry has been, and is now, a tremendous power for education and enlightenment among the Indians."[12] It is not surprising that Yellow Robe, like Charles Eastman, Carlos Montezuma, and countless other Indians became active in the Masons. Harold W. Shunk says that Chauncey "took the Entered Apprentice Degree of the Masonic Lodge on April 23, 1915; Fellow Craft Degree on May 16, 1915; Master Mason Degree on June 23, 1916; in the Rapid City Lodge No. 25. Chauncey received the Royal Arch Degree on July 6, 1917, in the Black Hills Chapter No. 25 in Rapid City; received the Cryptic Degrees in the Black Hills Council in Lead (South Dakota); in Schrader Commandery No. 9, Knights Templar, on November 11, 1917, in Rapid City."[13] While the exact requirements, meanings, and implications of each of these degrees, etc., might be known only to practicing Masons, it is clear that Chauncey approached this aspect of his life with the same vigor and enthusiasm that marked other endeavors.

15

Carlos Montezuma

A discussion of the American Indian Society would not be complete without some discussion of Chauncey's dealings with Carlos Montezuma. Of all of the relationships Chauncey Yellow Robe had with prominent Indian leaders, none is more interesting than that with Carlos Montezuma. They had a lot of things in common. They were both great believers in General Pratt and his work. They were both members of the Society of American Indians. They were both Masons. They were both married to white women. It is not surprising that they developed a close relationship and corresponded with each other often.

Wassaja (Carlos Montezuma) was born around 1866 in what became Arizona. As a young man this Yavapai Apache was taken captive by Pima warriors and sold to Carlos Gentile, a photographer. Gentile gave him his first name and then added the Montezuma as kind of a flourish and homage to his Mexican heritage. Montezuma eventually ended up in Urbana, Illinois. Working to pay his own way, he graduated from the University of Illinois and then went on to complete medical school at the University of Chicago Medical School.

Like Chauncey Yellow Robe, Montezuma's early career involved several moves while he worked with the Indian Service. He was the physician at Indian schools in North Dakota, Nevada, and the Colville Agency in the Pacific Northwest. As he moved from reservation to reservation he became aware and concerned about the worsening living conditions among the Indians. Shortly after taking the position at the Colville Agency in 1893 and remained there until 1896. He requested to be transferred to the Carlisle Indian School in Pennsylvania. It was while he was there that he met Chauncey Yellow Robe and started forming his ideas about the Indian situation and policy.

Pratt had been in communication with Montezuma for several years

15. Carlos Montezuma

before he came to Carlisle. He quickly bought into Pratt's ideas that the future of the Indian depended on the eradication of Indian ways by immersion in the white culture. Montezuma was a great ambassador for the school. He frequently praised all aspects of the school's program—its football team, its band, and most importantly its educational program. He was able to attend the Friends of the Indian Conferences at Lake Monhok. These conferences, held between 1883 and 1916, brought together a small group of wealthy eastern men and women who met annually to discuss American Indian policies. There he not only was exposed to new ideas but also to other Native American leaders and significant white movers and shakers.

Montezuma stayed at Carlisle until 1893 and then left the school to begin private practice. His Chicago practice was apparently not an overwhelming success. His interest in Native America affairs was rekindled, and he started to try to locate some of his relatives in Arizona. It was not long before Carlos Montezuma started to attach attention as an articulate, educated Indian leader. From that point on his life centered around Indian affairs and especially on creating some sort of an organization made up of Indians. He was articulate, focused to the point of being stubborn and witty—qualities that contributed to his reputation and standing.

Montezuma joined with other prominent native leaders, such as Charles Eastman and Henry Standing Bear, Arthur Parker, Laura Cornelius, Thomas Sloan, Rosa LaFlesche, Marie Baldwin, Henry Roe Cloud, Sherman Coolidge, Peoria Charles Daganett in preparing the way for the Society of American Indians—the first real pan–Indian organization. Like the others, Montezuma was a Pratt disciple and advocated assimilation. Unlike the others, he was afraid that the organization would soon become nothing but yet another tool of the Bureau of Indian Affairs.

The first real meeting of the Society of American Indians took place on Columbus Day, October 12, 1911, in Columbus Ohio. Despite his earlier involvement in laying the groundwork for the meeting, Montezuma chose not to attend. He decided to return to Arizona. In a November 11, 1911, letter to Montezuma, Yellow Robe writes that "I have no doubt you have had a pleasant vacation in Arizona."[1] Montezuma might not appreciate what he was doing in Arizona being characterized as a vacation. He was working there to try to prevent the federal government from relocating the Yavapai—the tribe of his birth. It was not easy, but the Yavapai won their case and they were permitted to stay at Fort McDowell. A couple of things developed as a result of his work in Arizona. First, he served notice to the Society of American Indians that he would not simply go along with them. Second, he served notice to the Bureau of Indian Affairs that he was not just another mild-mannered Indian who could be pushed around. The participants at the conference did not come dressed in tribal regalia. They wore business suits, spoke proper English, but most importantly, were convinced that what they were doing would usher in a new day in Indian affairs. Unfortunately, the seeds for the ultimate destruction of the S.A.I. were planted there as well. The attendees were in no sense representative of most American Indians. Twenty-one of the nearly thirty delegates were graduates or employees of Carlisle. The dominant force at the conference was Carlisle or schools like it. Accordingly, the specter of the Bureau of Indians Affairs was lurking as well. That is what bothered Montezuma. There seemed to be organizational issues as well. Chauncey wrote to Montezuma that "(since) the meeting has been closed without selection of permanent officers it cannot be considered as an organization." He added that he did not doubt that "the purpose of the intended Association means well enough but the alienation of (Charles) Daganett and the influences which combine to control for the interest of the Indian Bureau to keep the association silent behind the fence. Daganett has personal ambition before the Indian office—misrepresentation to his race. We have lots of such people in Indian deals."[2] So in one short letter Chauncey seems to ally himself with Montezuma with his concern about B.I.A. involvement, he questions the motives of his own employer, and he questions the motives of one of the movement's leaders. These are not the words of a timid or insecure man.

 Montezuma did not attend the 1913 S.A.I Conference in Denver. Owing at least in part to his absence, there was a much more upbeat and positive atmosphere. Chauncey called it "a great success."[3] Montezuma did attend and speak at the executive committee meeting that winter. Predictably, he was not quiet and unobtrusive. This time the focus of his attack was the Indian Schools. He decried such in-school activities as Indian basketry, Indian blanker, Indian pottery, Indian art, and Indian music. His question was "Where does this help the Indian children into the ways of civilization?" He evoked Jean-Jacques Rousseau by saying that the Indian "is born a blank, like the rest of us. What happens to him depends on his environment."[4] One might suspect that this would be "hit-

15. Carlos Montezuma

ting a little too close to home" for Chauncey, who had spent his adult life teaching in that very same Indian School system. Chauncey did reply but not in the way that one might suspect. He wrote to Montezuma, "The idea of teaching the Indian music in the Indian Schools is unprogressive—an un–American one. It is primarily an anthropological idea. Without the instruction of Indian music in the Indian Schools nearly every Indian child knows how to sing in their own mother tongue and this should be discouraged rather than encouraged."[5]

Montezuma became increasingly convinced that it was impossible, if not destructive, to try to work with the Indian Service. His definitive position, first made as a speech and later as a pamphlet, came in 1915 at the S.A.I. Conference in Lawrence. It was called "Let My People Go."

> Does this seem like a dream to you? Is your position a foreign attitude? From aloft, do you look down? Have you gone so far as to forget your race? Have you quenched the spirit of our fathers? As their children, dare we stay back, hide ourselves and be dumb at this hour, when we see our race abused, misused and driven to its doom? If this be not so, then let what ever loyalty and racial pride be in you awaken and manifest itself in this greatest movement of "Let My People Go!" The highest duty and greatest object of the Society of American Indians, is to have a bill introduced in our next Congress to have the Indian Bureau abolished and to let the Indians go. We cannot be disinterested in this matter, we cannot be jealous or hate one another, we cannot quibble or be personal in this matter. There must be no suspicion. We must act as one. Our hearts must throb with love—our souls must reach to God to guide us—and our bodies and souls must be used to gain our people's freedom. In behalf of our people, with the spirit of Moses, I ask this—The United States of America—"Let My People Go."[6]

Chauncey Yellow Robe and Carlos Montezuma were considered to be progressives in regard to Indian policy. Having the seemingly contradictory positions of advocating nearly total assimilation and still valuing and taking pride in being an Indian did not seem to bother them. Montezuma even moved close to saying that the Indian was in fact the superior race. Chauncey continued to work in the very same Indian School system he and Montezuma criticized. As the nation moved closer to the second decade of the twentieth century, they would find themselves disagreeing about Indian participation in World War I. Chauncey proudly proclaimed Indian patriotism and pointed out that Indians were being assimilated while many Europeans chose to keep their native culture and even language. Perhaps sarcastically Montezuma said that it might be a good idea to gather all Indians and then admit them to the United States as immigrants. The Indian policy of the federal government was nearly as complicated and convoluted as were the ideas of Indian progressives.

16

World War I

By the spring of 1917 Chauncey was comfortably ensconced as a pillar of the Rapid City Indian School, and he was well on his way be being recognized nationally as a perceptive and articulate spokesperson for American Indians. However, at that same time the world was far from being comfortable and was locked in a world war. On April 4, 1917, the United States formally entered that war—World War I, the Great War, the War to End All Wars. Less than a year before Woodrow Wilson had been reelected president with the slogan "He Kept Us Out of War." Suspicion and even paranoia had taken over and became the national norms. To that point Chauncey's life and focus primarily had been on the relatively isolated "worlds" of the reservation and boarding schools. That was about to change.

Few people know the extent of American Indian involvement in World War I either aboard or at home. Chauncey Yellow Robe and other American Indian leaders became immersed in a discussion that had five issues: why would American Indians fight in the war at all; can Indians be drafted; should the Indians be placed in segregated units; can the war be am Americanizing influence on Indians; is Indian participation proof positive that they deserved citizenship?

One explanation for the support Native Americans showed for the war might be misunderstood or even dismissed by whites. Major Brian J. Gilbertson, United States Marine Corps (an adopted member of the Ho-Chunk or Wisconsin Winnebago tribe), calls it the "warrior spirit." When World War I started the Indian wars were over. The only way these young men knew about them was through stories told by elders. "Warrior societies" still existed, but "The United States military had become, de facto, the only way an Indian can join the society of warriors."[1] This explanation should not be disregarded outright. The traditional responsibilities of

Chauncey Yellow Robe

Native warrior societies were leading hunts and raids, teaching the young the old traditions and rituals, caring for the elderly and those who could not care for themselves, punishing people who broke the law, and carrying out rituals. In the twentieth century the roles changed dramatically. They were carried out by formal tribal organizations and the state and federal government. Additionally, if the old rite of passage was participation in war no longer existed, it stands to reason that the military became the "de facto" warrior society as Gilbertson maintains.

There are other possible explanations for Indian participation in the war. On a very practical level, enlisting was a way to potentially escape the economic and social hardships of the reservations. It was a job and a comparatively high paying one. Food, shelter, and medical care were guaranteed.

The Bureau of Indian Affairs, which maintained an influential presence of reservations, worked enthusiastically to promote Indian participation in the war. Also it should be pointed out that native enlistment was overwhelming made up of young men who were students in the Indian School system.[2] These government schools operated in a very militaristic and stressed patriotic training. These schools had tremendous influence not only with the students but also with the alumni. They used the school newspapers to encourage young men to enlist. In his annual report Indian Affairs Commissioner Cato Sells said that Native American support of the war "was especially noticeable among the younger generation, largely the product of our Indian Schools."[3] Chauncey frequently talked about "my boys" (from Rapid City Indian School) who were in the military.[4] Carlisle reported that nearly sixty of its male students were in the military service. This accounted for nearly 1 percent of the total number of males at the school.[5] Additionally, with their affinity toward military education and vocational training, sometimes these young men were placed in more specialized jobs after they enlisted.

Finally, as Chauncey Yellow Robe would maintain, the Indians were patriotic Americans who loved their country and wanted to defend it. In his article "Indian Patriotism" Chauncey declared "We know that the "Indian Patriotism: has existed among the American Indians—as we see that they have demonstrated in this Great World War.... The American Indian is not lacking patriotism, he is not a disloyalist—a slacker or a traitor, but a true patriot.... In this war we see that the Indian has demonstrated his bravery and patriotism ... by patriotic motives thousands of

16. World War I

American Indians have gone forth to answer the call for service and now today they have engaged in every branch of the war service, that there are millions of dollars they have invested in the Liberty Bonds and thousands of dollars donated to the Red Cross and the Y.M.C.A. services."[6] Other prominent Indian leaders agreed. Arthur C. Parker, the leader of the Society of American Indians, said that "the Indian fights because he loves his freedom (and because) his country, his liberties, his ideals, and his manhood are assailed by the brutal hypocrisy of Prussiansm."[7]

In the 1918 Annual Report of the Commissioner of Indian Affairs, Commissioner Cato Sells supported the idea of expanding the evidence of patriotism to include those American Indians who supported the war effort but did not actually fight. "I reluctantly withhold a detailed account of the many instances of tribal and personal patriotism and of individual valor and achievement by our Indian soldiers in the service of both Canada and the United States that came to my attention during the year, for no record here would seem fittingly impartial that did not include the hundreds of noteworthy and authenticated incidents on the reservation, in the camps, and in France that have been almost daily recounted in the public prints. The complete story would be a voluminous narration of scenes, episodes, eloquent appeal, stirring action, and glorious sacrifice that might better be written into a deathless epic by some master poet born out of the heroic travail of a world-embattled era."[8] The degree of support for the war and the frequent displays of patriotism both in the military and on the home front, no doubt surprised many people.

Estimates vary about the number of Native Americans who were in the military in World War I. In 1918, the Commissioner for Indian Affairs reported that "after a systematic effort was made to procure reliable data as to the number enrolled for active duty by enlistment and draft, which is still incomplete, but sufficient for a close approximation, and justifies an estimate of 8,000 Indians now in training or actually in some branch of the Army and Navy. Of this number approximately 6,500 are in the Army, 1,000 in the Navy, and 500 in other military work. It is also significant that fully 6,000 of these entered by enlistment."[9] Most sources indicated that approximately 10,000 Indians served. This figure represents a significant percentage of the eligible adult male population. Native American participation was about .4 percent of the total number of soldiers during the course of the war. There is no reliable documentation to indicate how many Indians in the northern reservations enlisted in the Canadian army, and there were some who fought with France.

In June 1917, the federal government declared that all men between the ages of twenty-one and thirty-one needed to report to their local draft boards to register. In a decision that remains puzzling to this day, Native Americans also were required to register but not all of them were subject to the draft. The basis for that was that most Indians were not citizens. Only the specified ones could be drafted. The questions of how to register men who lived on remote reservations and how the process could be explained or communicated only added to the problem. Commissioner Sells determined that the Bureau of Indian Affairs should be responsible for registering the Indians and that on-site boards would be established on the reservations. More than one Indian asked the obvious question. Why should I register if I am exempt from compulsory service? Explaining that conundrum would be hard enough in English not to mention the numbers languages and dialects spoken by Native Americans. The additional problem of ascertaining exactly which Indians were citizens and subject to the draft proved to be confusing. In brief, it was decided that citizenship determination would be on a case-by-case basis. Commission Cato set and disseminated guidelines that would help:

>   1. Indians whose trust or restrictive fee patents were dated prior to May 8, 1906 were considered citizens as provided by the Dawes Act of 1887.
>   2. Indians whose trust or restrictive fee patents were dated prior to May 8, 1906 and who had received patents in fees for their allotments were considered citizens by virtue of the competency clause in the Burke Act.
>   3. Every Indian born within the territorial limits of the United States who had voluntarily lived apart from his people and had adopted the habits of civilized life was considered a citizen.
>
>   Minor children of parents who had become citizens upon allotment, and children born to Indian citizens were also considered American citizens.[10]

Using this system, over 6,500 Indians who registered were inducted. That was a little over half of the Indians who registered and an estimated 13 percent of the adult male population. Countless Indians thought that if they registered they would be drafted. It is not surprising that a few isolated instances of resistance or protest were reported. Each county had quotas they were expected to meet. These quotas applied to white and black young men separately if they resided in that county. Interestingly, for purpose of the distinction and quotas, Native Americans were counted

16. World War I

as whites. The result was that those counties with large numbers of American Indians could actually reduce the number of whites inducted.

The idea of drafting Indians was opposed by Carlos Montezuma. After he split with the Society of American Indians he published his own newsletter called *Wassaja*. In an article entitled "Drafting Indians and Justice," he wrote "Wassaja is not against the war nor against Indians going into the army if they so wish, of their own free will. But is it just to force them to be soldiers? Wassaja believes that this drafting of Indians into the army is another wrong perpetrated upon the Indian without FIRST bestowing his just title—THE FIRST AMERICAN CITIZEN. The legislature at Washington and the people of the United States may be ignorant of the awful imposition in which we, as true Americans, are imprisoned and enslaved. But WASSSAJA hopes that these words will stir up the patriotic feelings throughout these United States of America, so that the Indians will be made citizens. Then, and only then, can this country proudly draft them so that they will march side by side under the same flag with the brave patriots to victory truly, then, in behalf of THEIR COUNTRY."[11] To him the issue was simple. A Nation that did not give citizenship to Indians should not expect and ever demand that they sacrifice their lives to defend it.

Getting Native Americans into the military was not the only issue. Once there, something had to be done with them. The first and most intense debate about these new soldiers was whether they should be in segregated units like African American or integrated with whites.

The early voices for segregated units were not motivated by racism. Early advocates, like Joseph Dixon considered themselves preservationists rather than assimilationists. In 1917 Dixon actively lobbied Congress, the war Department, and the Bureau of Indian Affairs to keep the Indians separate from the whites in the military. Dixon believed that there were features of the Indian culture that needed to be preserved. He was an advocate of what he called the Native American "Cult of the Warrior,"[12] and said that separation would allow that feature of Indian culture to continue and feared that mixing the troops would inevitably bring the demise of the "noble traits" of the Indian. Although there was some support of his ideas, the assimilationists prevailed. Commissioner Sells saw integration as yet another step toward the culturalization. He had high powered support in this idea from the Society of American Indians, Richard Pratt, and Chauncey Yellow Robe. Chauncey and General Pratt corresponded several times about the issue.

Chauncey Yellow Robe

On April 7, 1917, he wrote to Pratt, "Your letter to the Secretary of War is all right and if your sound suggestion to enlist the Indians in the army can be carried out I have certain it will be success and if I can do any service in this matter I will be ready to answer the call. The war is on and this is the time for every able body Indian to participate in the service of his country to show that he is also a man and can help to prosecute this war."[13] Just a few days later, on April 15, 1917, Chauncey wrote that "I thank you for your wise suggestion as not to segregating the Indians in the army service. I assure you General I will not do anything that is contrary to your views. I know it will be unwise policy to organize companies or regiments of Indians for the service. I know that they will be known as Indian soldiers and not as American soldiers. If we are ever to become a part of this great nation we must be assimilated and to break the boundaries with the white men."[14]

Their feelings were shared by Commissioner Sells. In his 1918 annual report, he wrote regarding segregated units, "As to SEPARATE INDIAN ORGANIZATIONS. Early in the period covered by this report, I dissented from proposed encouragement of separate units of Indian soldiers in the Army as not in harmony with our plan for developing the Indian's citizenship … and I want the Indian to go into this conflict as the equal and comrade of every man who assails autocracy and ancient might, and to come home with a new light in his face and a clearer conception of the democracy in which he may participate and prosper."[15]

There were certainly examples of units made up entirely of Indians and there were problems, but was clear to many that, as Sells said: "War is a civilizer if from the blood and ashes of its battles flower the blessings of truth and enlightenment, although the fruit may be centuries in ripening." In words striking similar to Indian assimilationists, he goes on to say that "immediate benefit comes from the equal opportunity that they had with white comrades for gaining knowledge, for maturing judgment for developing courage through contact with events and conditions that trained and toughened character in defense of a just cause and a great ideal. No education serves a man better than this in any circumstance."[16]

Despite the calls for segregation of Indians in the military, the "Doughboys" themselves welcomed Native American soldiers. It was not for some altruistic reason but rather a practical one. The reputation of Indians as fierce fighters preceded them. After they were inducted the Indian soldiers went to training camps to prepare for war. Chauncey Yellow

16. World War I

Robe reported to General Pratt that "my boys are now at Camp Mills Long Island, N.Y. awaiting orders to sail for France. I wish I could be with them."[17]

For some of the new recruits this was the first time they had been away from the reservations. For some of them it was merely a continuation of the regime they were used to in boarding school. The training experience also brought whites and Indians together. For some, this was the first time that had happened. After the training the soldiers were sent to various points of embarkation. The long trip across the Atlanta brought a whole new set of anxieties for the Indians. Except for those "show Indians" who had accompanied Buffalo Bill and his Wild West show to Europe, this was the first time they had been on a trans-Atlanta trip. Compounding the problem of sea sickness, the soldiers had been warned about the lurking presence of German submarines. The first unites that had Indian soldiers reached France late in June 1917. From there, Native American soldiers took part in every major battle in Europe.

Chauncey proudly told General Pratt that some of his boys were part of the "famous Rainbow Division."[18] The 42 Infantry Division became known as the Rainbow Division when Douglas McArthur said that the division drew from 26 states and stretched across the nation like a rainbow. This division participated in six major campaigns including the Battle of Champagne in July 1918, in addition to fighting at Chateau-Thierry, St. Mihiel, Verdun and the Argonne.

Much was expected from the Native American soldiers. Many people saw them as natural soldiers who possessed a natural ability to develop and utilize complex strategies and maneuvers while being perfectly camouflaged. Others saw Indians as stoic, resolution fighting machines that were eager to fight and kill. It is not surprising that many of the Indian soldiers end up being scouts, snipers, and messengers. Given the nature of their duties, it is also not surprising that the percentage of Indian causalities was estimated to be 5 percent while the percentage of the American Expeditionary Force as a whole was 1 percent.[19]

There are countless stories of valor among the Indian soldiers. Following are only a few. Chauncey related the story about Sylvester Long Lance to General Pratt. In fact, Commissioner Sells told the same story in his annual report. According to Chauncey[20] Long Lance was a Carlisle graduate who was serving in the British army as a lieutenant. Commissioner Sells used Long Lance as an example of a brave Native American who enlisted the Canadian army in order to fight. Long Lane's acts of bravery and heroism became the fodder of the press and went a long way toward giving him a national reputation. Later he would earn another reputation because the war he told were largely fabrications, which were part of a grander scheme. Chauncey and Long would Lance cross paths later.

Thomas Britton says that "perhaps the most famous Native American hero in World War I was Private Joseph Oklahombi."[21] Joseph was a Choctaw from Oklahoma. Under a violent barrage, Oklahombi dashed to the attack of an enemy position, covering about 200 yards through barbed wire entanglements. He rushed on Machine Gun nests, capturing 171 prisoners." The press compared him to Sergeant Alvin York who received the Medal of Honor. Although they are not as well-known as the Navajo Code Talkers of World War II, Choctaw Indians were used by officers in the 142 Infantry Regiment, to convey messages over the telephone lines. Their language could not be decoded by the Germans.

In November 1921, President Harding dedicated the Tomb of the Unknown Soldier at *Arlington National Cemetery*. As an expression of a grateful nation Crow Chief Plenty Coos (or Plenty Coups) was invited to participate in the ceremony. He came dressed in full regalia. Plenty Coos addressed the crowd of dignitaries. "I am glad to represent all the Indians of the United States in placing on the grave of this noble warrior this coup stick and war bonnet, every eagle feather of which represents a deed of valor by my race. I hope that the Great Spirit will grant that these noble warriors have not given up their lives in vain and that there will be peace to all men hereafter."[22] Other officials, state and federal expressed their appreciation with lesser ceremonies and by sending certificates. The question now was not whether or not Indians should fight in the war, or even whether or not they could serve well. The question now was did their serve move them closer to earning (or being given) citizenship.

The question of Indian citizenship was not new. In fact, as mentioned previously, there were Indians who were citizens of the United States. But the vast majority of Native Americans were in a strange position of living in the United States while not being part of the United States, and that was not a bad thing for some of them. Chauncey Yellow Robe did not see it that way. To him, citizenship was a necessary element of assimilation. He said that the performance of Indian soldiers in the war should show the world that Native Americans were "entitled to citizenship."[23] Later in May 1919, he was even more direct when he wrote that "they have faced

16. World War I

the death side by side (with) the white man on the battle fields and so the Indians can face the duties of the American citizenship."[24] It might appear that the issue of citizenship and the rights thereof had already been addressed. After all Section 1 of the Fourteenth Amendment clearly states that

> All persons born or naturalized in the United States, and subject to the jurisdiction thereof, are citizens of the United States and of the state wherein they reside. No state shall make or enforce any law which shall abridge the privileges or immunities of citizens of the United States; nor shall any state deprive any person of life, liberty, or property, without due process of law; nor deny to any person within its jurisdiction the equal protection of the laws.

However, despite saying "all persons born or naturalized in the United States," the Fourteenth Amendment was designed to give citizenship to former slaves. Native Americans were not included. In 1884 the Supreme Court upheld that interpretation. Jim Elk was a Winnebago Indian who left the reservation to live in Nebraska as a white person. He tried to register to vote but was denied. The case got to the Supreme Court, and the Court declared that Elk was not subject to the jurisdiction of the United States since he was born in an "alien nation." His willingly giving up his tribal membership did not change things.

U.S. citizenship was not something Indians universally agreed upon or even wanted. In June 1919, Homer Snyder, a Representative from New York, introduced a bill that give citizenship to "every American Indian who served in the Military or Naval Establishments of the United States during the war against the Imperial German Government," if they had received an honorable discharge.[25] The bill and subsequent law did not actually give citizenship to Indian veterans .It gave those veterans the right to apply for citizenship—a process that was so cumbersome very few veterans applied. They were particularly troubled about giving up the "rights" and benefits that might be associated with their tribal membership.

In 1924, Snyder introduced another bill that old give citizenship to the approximately 125,000 non-citizen Indians. Addressing many of the Indians' concerns, that law stated:

> Be it enacted by the Senate and House of Representatives of the United States of America in Congress assembled, That all noncitizen Indians born within the territorial limits of the United States be, and they are hereby, declared to be citizens of the United States: Provided, That the granting of such citizenship shall

not in any manner impair or otherwise affect the right of any Indian to tribal or other property.

It was approved on June 2, 1924. The role that Native Americans played in getting that bill passed might be open to question. There were other political dynamics at play as well. There can be little question that, as Thomas Britten says, "(it) was the initial and perhaps most important catalyst for Indian citizenship."[26]

Chauncey Yellow Robe did not serve in the military during World War I or at any other time. He frequently expressed his remorse and frustration about not being able to be a part of this transformational event. Early in the war in June 1917 he seemed to have some hope for getting involved. In a letter to Pratt, June 21, 1917, he said that "my chances are doubtful now since the conscription act has gone into effect—of course there is always a way to first get into anything but I suppose my chances may come yet."[27] Later in November 1917, he wistfully wrote to Pratt that "I wish that I could be with them."[28] His age, his health, and his job at the Rapid City Indian School might have been disqualifiers, but clearly his heart and mind were with his boys. Ultimately Chauncey realized that his work at the school, the Society of American Indians, and the national stage he was ascending were where his efforts and energy should be spent.

Chauncey, the Rapid City Indian School, and the entire nation were about to realize that something had been brought home from the war that would challenge them and even kill thousands of them.

17

The Spanish Flu

Like most of the rest of the world, the Rapid City Indian School was infected and affected by the Spanish Influenza during the pandemic of 1918–1919. None of Superintendent House's reports or school records specifically mentions Chauncey Yellow Robe, but his position as disciplinarian would naturally put him squarely in the fray. Like so many others, he was felled by the flu. In a June 14, 1919, letter to General Pratt Chauncey wrote that "since October our whole school (closed) down with the 'flu,' and we lost six pupils. I had the 'flu' myself in October and for three weeks I had to fight for life."[1] In addition to the regular school employees, House was forced to hire special nurses and attendants who worked steadily through October and early November of 1918. Interestingly, and probably due to her own health and caring for her own children and Chauncey, Lillian Yellow Robe, although a nurse who had been employed at the school, is not listed among the 21 who were hired during this time period.

In March 1918, health officials in Haskell County, Kansas, sent a disturbing message to officials at the Public Health Service telling them about the appearance of a particularly virulent type of influenza at Fort Riley. At that time it was not required to report cases of "the flu," but this one scared the officials in Kansas. History would prove their concerns to be justified. Before it was over, the influenza pandemic accounted for the loss of over 600,000 Americans and over 20 million worldwide.

Conditions for the spread of the disease were ideal. The world was at war. Soldiers were traveling all over the world and were often crowded together in trains, ships, trucks, and barracks. The symptoms of what probably could have been more correctly identified as the Haskell County Flu instead of the Spanish Flu appeared quickly after exposure and ranged from mild to extreme. The disease was often referred to as *la grippe*—a romantic sounding French expression. Sometimes sufferers were simply sick for a few days and got better; sometimes they did not. What started out as fatigue, fever, and headache escalated, and the victims began coughing violently and uncontrollably. They coughed and spit bloody foam from their mouths; sometimes their ears and eyes bled; they became incontinent and vomited. The most serious affected victims' skin which turned blue, and often they died from resultant pneumonia. The country was barely mobilized for war and certainly not capable of dealing with the pandemic. In fact, the domestic war effort itself, along with its public rallies and bond drives contributed to the problem. The huge doses of home remedies such as kerosene and sugar, camphor, garlic, and sarsaparilla were powerless. In September 1918, the Navy Department distributed a detailed list of prevention and treatment suggestions and procedures. Included in these were the following:

> Protect yourself from infection, keep well, and do not get hysterical over this epidemic. Avoid being sprayed by the nose and throat secretions of others. Avoid crowded street cars—walk to the office if possible. Eat simple, nourishing food and drink plenty of water. Avoid constipation. Secure at least seven hours of sleep. Avoid physical fatigue. Keep the feet dry. If you become ill do not try to keep up with your work. Fight the disease rationally and do not become unduly alarmed.[2]

The first student evidencing the symptoms of the disease arrived on campus at Rapid City on September 22, 1918. The state of South Dakota reported its first official case the next day. Although they were accustomed to students dribbling in to start the year, it was clear to Superintendent House that this was not going to be the typical beginning of a new school year. Twelve days after the first case was reported at the school, Superintendent House wrote to the government farmer in the Blackpipe District that "I do not think conditions warrant anyone in staying out of school. I very much desire that all pupils come in promptly."[3] On that same day he received a letter from Henry Tidwell, superintendent of the Pine Ridge Agency.

> It has been reported in the Agency that your school is being visited with an epidemic of Spanish Influenza and that Rapid City has quite a few cases. This is to request that you advise me as to the facts in the case and whether in your opinion any of the Indians of the Reservation who have brought children to the school have been exposed to same. If there is an epidemic of this nature in Rapid City I request the authorities of said city to quarantine any residents of the Reservation and not allow them to return to this reservation. And you are requested to make this request of said city officials.[4]

17. The Spanish Flu

The next day House responded to Tidwell.

> This disease, diagnosed as Spanish influenza, made its appearance here about a week ago. Most of the cases have been of mild form, probably 15 cases in all here at the school. I have concluded it best to not take in any more pupils until there is an improvement in conditions. There are about 120 pupils here, will probably be 150 when those who are on the road arrive. I have also wired the railroad agents where I have placed tickets not to furnish any more transportation until further advised. In regard to quarantine of the Indians here, I fear it would be almost impossible, as the city authorities have not placed any restrictions on persons coming or leaving and they would probably not want to apply a quarantine to Indians that did not apply to others. The Indians being camped near the city, about two miles from the school could come and go without my knowledge. I am in hopes that this disease will subside before it reaches a serious state, but I must say that the outlook at present is not very encouraging.[5]

Within twenty-four hours, the situation changed dramatically for House. He changed from encouraging students to return to school to officially telling railroad agents to keep them away and not to transport them. While certainly possessing more information, another cause might be revealed further along in his letter to Tidwell when he reported that "(my) youngest daughter that has been working in the First National Bank was taken with it last night, and she is a mighty sick girl today. I would advise all parents that there [sic] children will have every care possible here, and they should not come to see them unless they are called."[6]

On that same day, October 5, Superintendent House wrote to the Commissioner of Indian Affairs: "I have gone over conditions with the school physician and with his recommendation have ordered all school work rooms closed, and will have no assembly of pupils other than is required for meals. I have also ordered that pupils be placed so as to have the smallest number possible in the various rooms and dormitories. I have arranged for keeping the pupils who are well in the open as much as possible. Teachers and other employees have been assigned to duties where needed."[7]

Although the medical care generally afforded the students was not great, House seemed to intuitively know the best ways to deal with this emergency. He moved quickly, decisively, and did so without first going through the time-consuming process of asking permission. At the same time, he was faced with the problem of having students already en route showing up at school. On October 8, he admitted nine students from Pine Ridge, and the attending physician was too busy to even examine the new arrivals. It was clear that controlling the comings and goings of the students would be difficult. House's friend and colleague C.J. Crandall, Superintendent at the Indian school in Pierre admitted as much in a letter to House on October 31. He said, "During the height of our epidemic, five of our children ran away. In fact there came very near being a panic as many were frightened."[8] Three days after closing the Rapid City school, Assistant Commissioner E.B. Merritt notified House that his action had been approved.

Closing the school did not alleviate the issue of caring for the students (House consistently referred to them as pupils) who were already there. The school employees were used to care for the sick and to try to prevent the well from getting sick. House told the Commissioner that the school's teachers and other employees were "doing all that can be asked and many of the employees are going beyond their strength."[9] As would be expected, many of them and their families became ill with the flu. In his official report to the Commissioner of Indian Affairs, Special Physician, Dr. L.L. Culp, reported that "Every employee was worked to death, but was whole heartedly interested and trying to exert every ounce of energy for the welfare of the sick. Volunteer nurses from the town of Rapid City saved the day by their extraordinary effort to relieve the lack of nurses. No pupil was neglected in any way, and no school of pupils ever received more individual care in an epidemic of any kind." Culp had been assigned, if not to coordinate, at least to report on how the different schools and agencies were dealing with the pandemic[10]

Superintendent House performed admirably throughout the epidemic, although he seemed at times to be conflicted—vacillating between doing what was best for his "pupils" and what was best for the school. He never expressed the emotions that his friend Crandall did when he wrote to House that, "we have lost 15 of our children. It has been hard on me and I am aging under the strain. It makes me feel like quitting, but I don't want to quit under the circumstances as at present."[11] And, in fact, despite the pressure of the situation, he seemed to have been a very gracious and accommodating host to Dr. Culp during his emergency visit to Rapid City. Culp wrote to House, "With kindest regard to yourself, family and all at Rapid City from both of us and assuring you that in our thoughts our short stay there will continue to be filled with pleasant memories."[12] In the face of such illness and death, it is hard to imagine that there could be many pleasant memories, but House was obviously a good host, and Culp

17. The Spanish Flu

was certainly complimentary in his report to the Commissioner of Indian Affairs.

Before the epidemic had substantially subsided, House was expressing concerns about the financial impact the epidemic might have on the school. Not only were they having to spend more money caring for the sick students, they were compiling attendance and enrollment figures that were very much lower than the previous year. As funding was per capita, House could see problems developing. By late October, he was writing the superintendents at the reservations, suggesting that the epidemic was just about over and that they should start getting the students there as quickly as it was safe to do so. He admitted to Superintendent Tidwell that, "the attendance here is much below our capacity, and I wish to fill up the school as soon as it seems safe to do so," and speculated to his friend Crandall that "as to managing this matter in the Indian Office as affects the per capita allowance. I have no idea as to what will finally be determined. We could, and I think the principal is carrying our absent pupils as on leave, but such a method could hardly be carried through the entire year and it now looks as if it would be very hard to fill the school."[13] He was clearly concerned about the funding issue and was looking for ways to handle what he anticipated would be Washington's response.

That response came, as House knew it would, in a letter from Assistant Commissioner Merritt. Coinciding with an uptick in flu cases in December, Merritt's letter of December 11, 1918, was not well-received. Merritt said, "Your monthly report for October is returned. You will note from examination thereof that the figures given in column four are high compared with the figures given in column five, resulting in a percentage of attendance of only 47.5. It is possible that the figures given in column four are incorrect in that they may include pupils who do not belong in school on the day in question, although duly enrolled at a prior time."[14] House's response was direct.

> Referring to your letter of the 11th instant, relative to the monthly report for October, I am returning this report herewith without change in the columns referred to. It will be observed that column four is greatly in excess of column five. This is due to the fact that column four includes pupils who were enrolled and who are constructively members of the school. However, owing to the fact that that the actual enrollment and attendance at the school were stopped on the 5th of October on account of the prevalence of Spanish influenza, the number actually attended for the month was reduced and this results in a low percentage of attendance.

Chauncey Yellow Robe

> In so far as I am able to get information, I am dropping all pupils from the enrollment who will not be able to return. Some of those who are out of school have died and some have married and other conditions will prevent some from returning. I am getting reports on these as rapidly as possible from the reservation superintendents and when it appears that a pupil cannot return I am dropping such from enrollment.
>
> The present attendance is set at 172. It is believed that there are 100 pupils that will be able to return should conditions become no worse than at present. This would bring the actual attendance up to about 275, which would be as many as we could well accommodate.[15]

Indeed there is some evidence that House did communicate with the reservation superintendents about rounding up those who had not attended or had left, but it is equally evident that he deferred to their judgment, and in most cases, the superintendents felt it would be unwise to repopulate the school at this time. House then sought assistance from The U.S. Representative from the area around Rapid City, Democrat Harry L. Gandy.

> I presume it has already been brought to your attention that the Indian schools in South Dakota have been very much disturbed as to attendance by the epidemic of influenza. Our attendance here is very much below the usual, and it is doubtful whether it can be brought up to the usual number; although, there are a good many pupils out that I expect will come in after the holiday season. Whatever the result may be, will not be a per capita attendance based on the attendance of the four quarters of the year that will be sufficient to utilize the entire appropriation, and I presume the other schools of the state are in the same condition? There would seem to be no remedy except by act of Congress, and I presume you have had this matter already presented to you.[16]

Whether House eventually succumbed to the pressure of re-enrolling students or not is certainly open to conjecture. What is clear is that by reopening the school, several students were exposed or re-exposed to the Spanish flu. There were reoccurrences in February 1919. House wrote to the Commissioner, "Referring to correspondence relative to influenza epidemic, I have to advise that since second appearance of this disease we have had 20 cases in all, five of which have been second attack. One case is showing a tendency toward tuberculosis, and while it is not expected that this case will terminate fatally, I presume it will be necessary to dismiss the patient from further attendance at school."[17]

By the time the Spanish flu had run, and unexpectedly rerun its course at the Rapid City Indian School, at least six students on the campus had

17. The Spanish Flu

died.[18] The exact number of students who died is difficult to determine since many were staying in camps outside of the city, and others had been unable to report to the school. Subsequently, the school was "plagued" with diminishing enrollment and financial problems. Scott Riney said, "The school's greatest failing was its inability to provide adequate health care for students."[19] Cases of trachoma, measles, scarlet fever and even small pox were reported among the students.

While the epidemic and other health related issues did not directly bring about the demise of the school, they were contributing factors. The facility was briefly converted to a tuberculosis sanatorium hospital for students in 1929. It changed back to a regular boarding school in 1930 and was finally closed in 1933. In 1939, it reverted to a tuberculosis sanatorium—the Sioux Sanatorium. Now the property and the few original buildings that remain house the Indian Health Services. Soo San (Sioux Sanitarium) Drive is still there, and the property is still very much in the news. Two Rapid City residents, Kibbe Conti (Oglala Lakota) and Heather Dawn Thompson (Cheyenne River Sioux), began doing research to try to locate unmarked graves of children who died at the school. Their research led to an in-depth history of the roughly 1,200 acres the school originally owned. They traced the transfer of portions of the property after the closing of the school. An organization called the Mniluzahan Okolakiciyapi Ambassadors (50 percent Native and 50 percent non-native) has produced a presentation called "An Inconvenient Truth: The History Behind Sioux San Lands and West Rapid City" intended to foster more dialogue and relationships between the city's white and Native populations. The first slide in that presentation was the before and after picture of Chauncey, Richard, and Henry Standing Bear made at Carlisle.

18

Wounded Knee and Wild West Shows

Big Foot was by nature a cautious and deliberate man. That was part of the reason he was valued as a negotiator. So, when the nephew of Sitting Bull (Tatanka Iyotake) came to the Cheyenne River camp and reported that his uncle had been killed, Big Foot was skeptical and yet worried. However, when his scouts returned and confirmed the report and when several of the Hunkpapa followers of Sitting Bull started drifting into the camp, Big Foot knew that it was true, and he knew that is was time to act—but not to fight Colonel Stanton, who had "captured" Big Foot and the Minneconja just days before. Nor was it a good idea to flee to the Badlands and join the Stronghold Sioux as others feared but rather to move to Pine Ridge and join Red Cloud. He had been asked to bring his negotiating skills to Pine Ridge already, but now there was urgency and even fear involved in his decision making.

The U.S. Army was never quite sure how a sick old man and some 300 people in a sorry assortment of makeshift wagons could slip away without being detected, but it happened during the night of December 23, 1890. When the Army discovered they had left, word was sent to Major Whiteside in Pine Ridge, and he positioned his soldiers at the village of Wounded Knee to intercept the Minneconja.

Big Foot sat wrapped up in blankets in an old wagon. Blood dripped from his nose and pooled on the floor. Each rattling cough brought another wave of excruciating pain to his chest and back. They had traveled a nearly incomprehensible fifty miles in two days. He was suffering from pneumonia, and each bump of the wagon seemed to dislodge a bit of his life. He was dying, and he knew it. The Army knew they were coming; sick people, old men, women children, and thrown together wagons make being stealth

18. Wounded Knee and Wild West Shows

difficult. Despite that, Big Foot's scouts surprised the Army's scouts at Porcupine Creek on December 28. When they were taken to Big Foot, he told them that the Minneconja did not intend to fight. As soon as they finished eating they would be coming on to Wounded Knee. That was the path he chose, and that would be the path they took. Not all of the Sioux thought that was the best course of action, but that was the way it was going to be. When the scouts returned to the Army's camp, Major Whiteside quickly requested reinforcements. The Second Battalion of the Seventh Cavalry under Colonel James Forsyth came from Pine Ridge.

As the Indians approached, the U.S. Army prepared. Weapons were posed and the awesome Hotchkiss guns were positioned. Forsyth found Big Foot to be gravely ill and ordered him transferred to a more comfortable army ambulance. Big Foot agreed and continued to stress that the Indians did not intend to fight. The soldiers judiciously surrounded the Indian band, and talks slowly started. There was an air of uneasiness on everyone's part. Inexperienced and possibly intoxicated soldiers were poised around nervous and distrustful Indians. Matters got worse when the Army demanded that the Indians surrender their weapons. Although they had weapons, most were old and unreliable. Those with newer, better rifles were loath to give them up. The first batch that was collected did not satisfy the Army, so other roundups ensued. Knives, cooking utensils, and a few newer, operative weapons were discovered. The Army then started searching under the robes the frigid Indians were wearing. Off to the side, a medicine man named Sits Straight or Good Thunder started an impromptu Ghost Dance. Ironically, the Ghost Dance, which was purportedly the reason the Army was in Indian country, went largely unnoticed. One nearly deaf Indian named Black Fox or Black Coyote resisted giving up his rifle. The gun went off, and the carnage began.

Nearly half of the Indians were killed in the first massive volley. The Army's positioning, which seemed to make so much sense earlier, became a liability. Many soldiers positioned across from each other were killed by friendly fire. The Indians responded as best they could with knives, clubs, and fists. The adage, the only good Indian is a dead one, seemed to be the rule of the day. Fleeing Indians, women, and children, were killed. Some were found dead nearly two miles away from Wounded Knee. It was all over pretty soon. A cloud of smoke hung over the massacre field. The word battle simply did not apply.

Overnight, the onset of the cold South Dakota winter transformed the bodies into macabre frozen statues. Contract workers from Pine Ridge dug a mass grave, and the slaughtered Indians were buried. Reportedly, Big Foot was the third Indian placed in the grave. The exact number of Indians killed at Wounded Knee on December 29, 1890, is hard to determine. The estimates range from slightly over 100 to over 300. However, one documented death was that of a person simply identified on the marker as Yellow Robe.

Chauncey was incensed when he learned that Buffalo Bill Cody was making a movie that included scenes from the massacre at Wounded Knee. He was bothered even more by the fact that the film was endorsed and even supported by the U.S. Army and the Department of the Interior. He delivered a speech at the Society of American Indians conference in Madison, Wisconsin, in which he said:

> Before the closing history of the nineteenth century, an awful crime was committed in this great Christian nation. It was only a few days after the nations of the world had celebrated the message of the heavenly host [at Christmas] saying, "Fear not, for behold I bring you good tidings of great joy which shall be to all people"; and "Glory to God in the highest and on earth peace good will toward men." A band of Sioux Indians, including women and children, unarmed, were massacred. The wounded were left on the field to die without care by the United States troops just because they had founded a new religion called "The Indian Messiah." This was a cowardly and criminal act without diplomacy.
>
> Twenty-three years afterward, on the same field of Wounded Knee, the tragedy was reproduced for "historical preservation" in moving picture films and called "The Last Great Battle of the Sioux." The whole production of the field was misrepresented and yet approved by the Government.
>
> This is a disgrace and injustice to the Indian race. I am not speaking here from selfish and sensitive motives, but from my own point of view, for cleaner civilization, education, and citizenship for my race.[1]

One thing that especially irked Yellow Robe was the mistaken understanding that Buffalo Bill himself and General Nelson Miles were both depicted in the film as being present and heroes at Wounded Knee. Chauncey is quoted in a newspaper article as saying that they "went back and became heroes for a moving picture machine ... they want to be heroes for moving pictures. You will be able to see their bravery and their hairbreadth escapes soon in your theaters."[2] In fact, the reenactment of the massacre at Wounded Knee was only a small part of a grander project entitled *The Indian Wars*. The attempt to reconcile Buffalo Bill's theatrics

18. Wounded Knee and Wild West Shows

with the official United States government's description of a series of battles between the army and the Indians generated its own bizarre story.

Not very long after Thomas Edison publically demonstrated the kinetoscope in 1893, Buffalo Bill and his Wild West Show performers visited the inventor at his studio in West Orange, New Jersey. Never one to pass up an opportunity for publicity and exposure, Buffalo Bill and his performing Indians posed for pictures that showed an Indian war council, complete with a peace pipe, and a demonstration of Bill's rapid fire prowess. Some twenty years later, in a last-ditch effort to breathe new life into both his career and finances, Buffalo Bill decided to make a movie chronicling his own life. He had been unable to repay a loan of $20,000 to Harry Tamman and Fred G. Bonfils, who were co-owners of the Sells-Floto Circus and the *Denver Post*. The property of the once worldwide hit show was sold at auction. Bonfils and Tamman believed that Buffalo Bill still had enough draw to make a little more money for them. They joined with Cody in establishing The Colonel William F. (Buffalo Bill) Cody Historical Pictures Company and enlisted financial supporters and technical advisors from the movie industry to begin the project. Although he had made no financial contribution himself, Cody was given a one-third interest in the film and was to be given a copy of the completed film for posterity.

The project received considerable early praise. Not only would it be an exciting portrayal of an American legend, it would also be historically accurate. The Secretary of War Department, Lindley M. Garrison, agreed to permit soldiers from the Twelfth Cavalry to serve as extras, and the secretary of the Interior, Franklin Lane, agreed to allow Indians from Pine Ridge to be in the movie as well. The movie would recreate the battles of Summit Springs, "Custer's Last Stand," Warbonnett Creek, and the Wounded Knee Massacre. While carefully crafted product placement would not appear in movies for many years, it was clear that the government intended for it to be a vehicle for promoting the good works of the U.S. Government regarding the Indians. The superintendent of the Pine Ridge Agency, John Brennan, was instructed to be sure that there was footage that included "pictures of the (Indian) children in school working and on the farm and otherwise industrially engaged."[3] The intent was to present a positive picture of the government's work.

Most of the filming of the movie took place in the fall of 1913, and controversy surrounded it from the outset. A great deal of it dealt with the decision to use the actual Wounded Knee site for the filming of that part of the movie. Cody was staying with friend and business associate James E. Asay in Rushville, Nebraska, during the filming of the parts that took place at Pine Ridge and felt that the use of Wounded Knee would only contribute to the film's authenticity—especially since some actual Indian participants would be in the movie. Of equal or even more concern was the fact General Miles was certainly not pleased with the army's handling of the massacre. In his autobiography, he said that "I have never felt that the action was judicious or justified, and have always believed that it could have been avoided."[4] During the filming itself, Miles wisely remained sequestered in the village of Pine Ridge. However, apparently in whatever forms the film finally ended up, Miles seemed to have approved. He wholeheartedly endorsed it as being historically correct after a private viewing in Chicago on January 21, 1914. The film was shown twice in Washington, D.C.—first to the National Press Club and then at an event hosted by the Department of the Interior.

The Indian Wars made its official premiere in Denver on March 8. As might be expected, the *Denver Post* gave it a favorable review calling it a film "the like of which we have never seen before."[5] It soon appeared in other cities including Omaha, Alliance, and Chadron, Nebraska, and Milwaukee, Wisconsin. A negative publicity campaign was developing at the same time. Chauncey was joined in his condemnation of *The Indian Wars* by Dr. Melvin Gilmore, noted ethnologist and curator of the museum of the Nebraska State Historical Society. Gilmore called the film "a disgrace to the government under whose sanction it was made."[6] Gilmore had interviewed massacre survivors and had written about the incident at length.

C. Ryley Cooper, a writer for the *Denver Post* who apparently actually saw the film being made, said that "There (at Wounded Knee) the white man was the aggressor, they far outnumbering the Indians. The red men were crowded down into a great ravine where lines of bullets sent them to death in score."[7]

Perhaps owing to the government's concern about the Army's appearance in the film as being the aggressor or due to the apparent lack of public interest in seeing an aged Buffalo Bill playing himself fifty years younger, the film quickly and almost totally disappeared. The government's copies, which were to be kept as historical records, are unaccounted for, and all of the original film that seems to remain is a two minute snippet that is preserved at the Buffalo Bill Historical Center in Cody, Wyoming. Whether Chauncey ever saw the film or if his concerns were justified remains

18. Wounded Knee and Wild West Shows

unknown. What is known is that he openly advocated the accurate and fair depiction of American Indians in the emerging medium of film.

The decline in the popularity of the wild west type of shows in the United States was not evident in other parts of the world. Owing in large degree to the popularity of American frontier novels by authors in France and Germany, the fascination with American Indians continued for decades. In France, Gustave Aimard (Olivier Gloux) serialized several adventure novels set in the United States and featuring a strong American Indian presence and influence. The German Karl Friedrich May was arguably the most popular and influential frontier novelist. His thousands of readers were convinced that he had lived the adventures he wrote about in books like *Winnetou*, the story about an Apache chief and his white blood brother, Old Shatterhand.

The Sarrasani Circus, established by Hans Stosch-Sarrasani, began touring Europe with over twenty Oglalas, around 1912. The onset of World War I created an unanticipated crisis for these "show Indians." Undocumented as they were, they were detained in Hamburg as Serbian spies. The America counsel secured their release and they fled to London. The circus and its performing Indians resumed touring after the war. It was reported that the more affluent Europeans were given the opportunity to actually touch the Indians for the right price.

The grave of Edward Two Two, an Oglala Lakota from South Dakota, is located in a cemetery in Dresden, Germany. Two Two came to Germany as a show Indian, on display first at a "human zoo" and later joined the Sarrasani circus. When he died in 1914, he was buried there. The Two Two name is still a prominent one on the Pine Ridge Reservation, and many graves of Two Twos are found in Wounded Knee Cemetery.

Recently, Ojibwa representatives have requested that scalps currently on display at the Karl May Museum be returned to the tribe. These scalps were purchased from the tribe in 1904 by Ernst Tobias for a reported $1,000 and three bottles of alcohol. They were bequeathed to the museum. The museum claims not to know the exact tribal affiliation of the scalps but reports that at least two were white people. That conversation is ongoing at the time of this writing. The Museum's most recent response says that it is "Shocked and also surprised by your accusations because it has never been and never will be the Karl May Museum's aim to show disrespect to any Native American or First Nations culture.... The scalp which is said to be of Ojibwa heritage and that you probably are referring to, has

Chauncey Yellow Robe

not been on display at the Karl May Museum for 20 years and it is being kept safe in our depot right now. There is only one source labeling the scalp to be of an Ojibwa and the origin of this information is not proven. Neither is any classification and provenience of the scalps that are part of the Karl May Museum's collection clear, nor do we have any scientific verification concerning their authenticity.... If you saw our exhibition (which does contain human remains) you would know that there is a special focus on the misuse of scalps (scalp premiums). To us, this show case has a memorial character to the past when white settlers and trappers did not think anything of human rights."[8]

Chauncey Yellow Robe's concern that Native American culture be accurately and authentically represented and not viewed as simply a cultural curiosity is still present among Native Americans. Recently controversies about derogatory caricatures and representations, sports teams' mascots, and the casual wearing of traditional clothing and headdress by non–Indians are examples of issues that large numbers Native Americans feel strongly about today.

19

The Silent Enemy

"Hau" *[How]*
  This picture is the story of my people. I speak for them because I know your language. In the beginning the Great Spirit gave us this land. The wild game was ours to hunt. We were happy when game was plenty. In years of famine we suffered.
  Soon we will be gone. Your civilization will have destroyed us. But by your magic we will live forever. We thank the white men who helped us make this picture. They came to our forest. They share our hardships. They listened to our old men around the campfire. We told them the stories our grandfathers told us. That is why this picture is real.
  Look not upon us as actors. We are living our own life today as we lived it yesterday. Everything you see is as it always has been: our buckskin clothes, our birch bark canoes, our wigwams, and our bows and arrows. All were made by my people just as they always have done.
  Only six of these Indians have ever seen a motion picture. Many of them are still in the forest, hunting game that is ever growing less. Still they feel the great drummer of the North, this struggle for meat, a never-ending fight against the silent enemy.
  Chauncey "Chief" Yellow Robe in *The Silent Enemy*[1]

In the late 1920s, what were the chances that Chauncey Yellow Robe, the grandson of Russian author Leo Tolstoy, a University of Pennsylvania student who moonlighted as a vaudeville dancer, a trustee from the American Museum of Natural History, and a North Carolina man of mixed blood masquerading as a Blackfoot chief would come together in the wilderness of northern Ontario? The project that brought this unlikely group together was the filming of *The Silent Enemy*, a silent movie docudrama showcasing the Ojibwa Indians' struggle for food during a pre–Columbian winter.

Chauncey Yellow Robe

To put things in perspective with regard to this groundbreaking movie, it is important to remember that for almost 50 years prior to its release in 1930, Indians had been exploited for the entertainment of Europeans and Americans. From medicine shows and wild west productions that "re-enacted" famous Indian battles and featured riding and shooting exhibitions, to the 1890s' silent films that portrayed racial stereotypes in the extreme. Before D.W. Griffith filmed *Birth of a Nation* in 1915, he made approximately 30 short melodrama films featuring Native American characters for the Biograph Company. Hundreds of documentaries and shorts were produced by other film makers, and in general, these efforts were wildly popular, even though Indians were played by white men in "red face," much as blacks had been portrayed in black face early on.

There were several reasons that these movies were popular. First, Indians were familiar enough from 19th century history, songs and dime novels to be recognized, but still exotic enough to be mysterious and dangerous. Riding horses, fighting, burning homes and threatening white women made for visual impact in the growing world of cinema. There are estimates that 50 Indian movies were released in 1909 and an average of 150 films each year after that, through 1914. Ward Churchill has expanded that estimate to suggest that over 2000 films and well over 10,000 television shows have featured American Indians since the end of the nineteenth century.[2]

Second, most of these movies were melodramas, pitting clear good against evil, the noble against the scoundrel. The characters were exaggerated and the plots were formulaic to elicit great emotion from the audience. Many of these shorts portrayed the Indians as the victims of white man's greed and deception.

Third, women played significant roles in Indian films, patterning "squaws" after historical females (Pocahontas) and fictional ones (Minnehaha). Damsels caught in forbidden love, cultural conflict or plain, old-fashioned distress made for romance, sacrifice, or drama.

Fourth, late in the 19th century, anthropologists sounded the alarm about the fast disappearing Native American culture as the frontier was closed. Mainstream America expected the Indians to disappear altogether, or, if not, their image to remain frozen as in earlier days. The stereotypical war paint, wampum belt, and tipis would not give way to changes in society. It was difficult, if not impossible, for many Americans to see American Indians doing all of those everyday things they did.

19. The Silent Enemy

American citizens were able to go to the movies and get caught up in the lives and struggles of the Indian characters, whether played in red face or, later, by genuine Indians, but may not have connected those stories to actual events that were taking place: Sitting Bull's death at the hands of the reservation police, the Cavalry's slaughter of 150 to 300 men, women and children at Wounded Knee, both in 1890.

Cheering for a single noble savage in a love story did not mean sympathy for Native Americans in general. Weeping for a self-sacrificing squaw who gives up her white true love because of strong tribal connections was separate from the dissolution of all tribes through the Dawes Act of 1887. Audiences who wept as mothers were separated from children in the movie had little understanding of the actual impact of relocated reservation and boarding schools Native children were forced to attend. During the first 10 years of the 20th century, the movie plots began to reflect changes in the way the Indian was perceived. Nostalgia gave way to fear and hostility.

Although it was neither as artistic nor as authentic as Edward Curtis' groundbreaking *In the Land of the Head-Hunters* in 1914, *The Silent Enemy* has been recognized as an important and poignant film representation of Indian life. Being predominantly silent and coming close to the end of that era, *The Silent Enemy* was not extremely popular or well-received at the time. However, more recently it is frequently featured at silent movie festivals. Benjamin Schrom wrote this about the movie after it played at the San Francisco Silent Film Festival in 2008:

> Seeking to correct the spurious and demeaning image of Native Americans in mainstream films, Burden and Chanler attempted to film only aboriginal people, their tools and their activities, in their actual habitat. Some of their achievements in this regard are staggering. Filming into the harsh Canadian winter, the cast and crew lived exclusively in teepees. Burden himself shared a teepee with Chief Yellow Robe. All the hunting implements and crafts shown in the film were made on the set by local Ojibway Indians, and many were exhibited at the American Museum of Natural History. Warren Iliff, director of the National Zoological Park, claimed 40 years after the film's release that "without qualification, the wildlife photography is the best I've ever seen" and, no doubt to the shock of an as-yet uninvolved SPCA, many animals were in fact harmed in its filming.[3]

The issue of authenticity was one that Yellow Robe took seriously. He had railed against Buffalo Bill's movie representation of the Wounded Knee Massacre and certainly would have knowingly had no part in any production that was not true to Indian life and struggles. The film was not intended to represent his life, but rather to represent the lives of ancestors and other Native Americans on the continent.

It was in this milieu of fading Native authenticity and exploitation, that William Douglas Burden wanted to make a film about the primitive life of the American Indians before Columbus arrived. He wanted to document the Ojibwa way of life and create a realistic portrayal rather than the Hollywood stereotype. He had the knowledge, experience and connections to make it happen. As an explorer and adventurer, Burden had grown up in a wealthy family, and had enjoyed times at his family's camp near Bear Creek in remote Quebec, where his father hunted and fished to relieve the stress of his job as president of Burden Iron in Troy, New York. The young Burden had been well educated at Groton and Harvard, but in the wilds with his father's hunting guide, Archie Miller, he learned his life's passion: adventuring in interesting places all over the world.

After hunting in Alaska, diamond mining in Brazil, tracking tigers in Indochina and ibex in the Himalayas, bringing back Komodo "dragon" lizards from the Dutch East Indies, and fresh off a new appointment as a trustee of the Natural History Museum, Burden presented his idea for a film to his Harvard classmate, William Chanler, an attorney in New York.

The story was to follow a band of Ojibwa Indians in Northern Ontario as their food sources are reduced and they travel into more unforgiving lands in search of herds of caribou to avoid starvation. Within the drama of the hazardous journey and the death of many, there is a sub plot of Neewa, the chief's daughter, who is loved by two members of the band—Baluk, the best hunter, and Dagwan, the sneaky medicine man.

Burden was influenced by a few other semi-documentaries of the time, such as *Chang* by Meriam Cooper and Ernest Schoedsack, which was the 1927 story of a Thai family who struggles for survival in the jungles of Southeast Asia. The film was nearly overwhelming to Burden with its landscapes and wildlife scenes He and fellow Harvard graduate and friend William Chanler took their ideas and a partially completed script to an executive at Paramount, Jesse Laskey, who agreed to distribute the film when production was complete. Count Ilia Tolstoy served as an assistant director and organized and led the expedition more than a thousand miles north of the railroad in order to identify the most likely crossing grounds of the caribou. This enabled the team to capture film of the impressive migration for the movie.

19. The Silent Enemy

The Silent Enemy was not going to be just another cowboy and Indian film. Burden immersed himself in research. He visited potential sites to do the filming. He hired H.P. Carver, a capable director, who had made movies about Indians before. Although he surely was not patterning his efforts after those of Buffalo Bill, he did hire actual Ojibwa Indians as extras in the movie. Burden was committed "to hiring only Indians." Burden was by no means the first producer to cast Indians as Indians. But he was one of a handful concerned about tribal specificity and the ethnographic correctness of clothing and props

To that end, Father Evain, a missionary in Canada for 40 years, helped secure the trust of the Indians who worked on the film. Many knew him or knew of him from his visits to villages over the years. He called the Indians "My Little Children of the Woods," and they welcomed him on his visits to the filming sites. Interestingly, the Ojibwas were actually experiencing many of the problems that were later depicted in the film at that time, and they signed up for the bit parts and meager salaries in large numbers. Casting the major roles would be a more exacting job. "Real" Indians frequently had roles as extras, but none had been called on to be a featured star. The controversy and interest generated by the film did not come from the broader issue of the authenticity of its plot and action, but to the legitimacy and back-story of the actors in it. Interestingly, more has been written about the other "stars" of the movie, Chief Buffalo Child Long Lance and Molly Dellis Nelson or Molly Spotted Elk, than about Chauncey Yellow Robe. Both have been subjects of biographies—unlike Yellow Robe who has not been, until this book.

The director, Carver, was able eventually to cast the three lead roles. He happened to meet Chauncey while both were viewing the Native American exhibits at the American Museum of Natural History in New York. The fact that he was identified as a great-nephew of Sitting Bull might have sealed the deal, but Carver was impressed that not only did Chauncey have "the look," but he also had the credibility of a person who had hunted buffalo and lived the life of a Plains Indian. He was a natural to fill the role of the wise, but old and dying, chief—Chetoga. The part of the chief's beautiful daughter, Neewa, was to be played by Molly Spotted Elk, or Molly Nelson (Molly Dellis Nelson Archambaud), an established performer who danced nightly at the Texas Guinan Night Club—one of the speakeasies run by Mary Louise Cecilia "Texas" Guinan, the queen of New York nightclubs.[4] The male lead, the role of Baluk, was offered to Chief

Chauncey Yellow Robe

Buffalo Child Long Lance—an author and well-known celebrity who, like numerous personalities of our time, was famous for being known. Baluk was, according to the script, "the epitome of manly development," and the rival for Neewa's affection with Dagwan, the evil medicine man. Long Lance fit the bill. *Screenland* magazine called him the "Chief of heart breakers,"[5] and he was an imposing figure.

Both Chauncey and Chief Buffalo Child Long Lance had attended Carlisle. Chauncey graduated in 1895. Long Lance had attended between 1909 and 1912. Chauncey, Kills in the Woods, went to Carlisle with a group of students taken from the reservations in South Dakota. Chief Buffalo Child Long Lance, Sylvester Clark Long, was accepted into Carlisle upon the recommendation and questionable application submitted by his father and the principal at the West End School in Winston-Salem, North Carolina, where Sylvester's father, Joe Long, worked as a custodian. The racial identity of the Longs was complicated. Joe claimed to be of Eastern Cherokee blood. Sylvester's mother claimed to be half Indian. She claimed an affiliation with the Croatan or Lumbee tribe. Neither was registered with their respective "tribes," but Sylvester's application to Carlisle indicated that his father was half Cherokee and his mother was half Lumbee—both were exaggerations. However, the undocumented claims were enough to get his application reviewed. There was also that little problem with his age. At the time of application, he was nineteen, and Carlisle did not admit students over eighteen. Already having stretched the truth about his Indian blood apparently made it easier lie some more, and they chopped a year off of his age. So, at age nineteen, this young man from North Carolina where his family was never considered anything but black, was admitted to Carlisle Indian School.

Long's "Indianness" was often questioned at Carlisle by Eastern Cherokees who had never seen or heard of him or his family. He was often ridiculed and even called the Cherokee "nigger" by the other students. Whatever his issues with the truth, Long was unquestionably strong and determined. Interestingly, it was at Carlisle, where Indian names were rejected or changed in favor of whiter names—like Chauncey, that Long was either informally given or assumed the name Sylvester Chahuska Long Lance, in order to seem more Indian. Long was certainly not content to merely blend into the background at Carlisle. Not only was he an outstanding student, but he also was involved and a leader in many school activities. Despite claims he made later in life, he did not make the varsity

19. The Silent Enemy

football team, but he was a good and lifelong friend of famed Carlisle athlete Jim Thorpe. He worked in the print shop and did his outing experience at the Cornman Printing Company in Carlisle. In 1910, he wrote an article that was published in *The Red Man* ironically titled "Origins of Names among the Cherokees."[6]

Just as he had learned some things about being an Indian from his brief stints earlier in life in the circus and Wild West show, Long learned from his Indian classmates at Carlisle. He graduated from the school in 1912 and applied to Conway Hall, the Dickinson College preparatory school in Carlisle. There he found himself a man, twenty-one years old, living and going to school with boys, and within a year he was ready to move on.

The next stop in his educational odyssey was at St. John's Military Academy, one of the most prestigious schools in New York. He was well-received there, and the "Chief" flourished. He was the focus of much attention and even adulation—quite different from Carlisle where his "Indianness" was always open to scrutiny. At St. John's he decided that his next step would be to apply for a presidential appointment to West Point. To facilitate that, he chopped a couple of more years off of his age and continued to say that he was born in western North Carolina on the Qualla Boundary. Perhaps to avoid the increasingly close scrutiny he might be facing from the War Department, Long did not pass the entry examination. In an ironic way, this suspiciously deliberate failure led to the full throttle growth of the Buffalo Child Long Lance legend.

Like many adventurous Americans, Long Lance got caught up in the excitement and romance of the Great War. He went to Montreal and enlisted in the Canadian Expeditionary Force on August 4, 1916. True to form, when an application was required, Long Lance saw an opportunity to embellish. He listed West Point as previous military experience. Before he left for action in France, he sent a poem to his friends at Carlisle.

> I've just come out of the trenches
> Where we made the Germans dance,
> And I am sending this Greeting to let you know
> That he is still alive, Yours Truly, Lieut. Long-Lance;
> Alive and fit as fit can be,
> Though fighting's not all sport,
> And manners "made in Germany"
> Aren't quite what you and I were taught.[7]

Chauncey Yellow Robe

When he finally did see action, he was injured twice and left the army as an acting sergeant. Long Lance stayed in Canada and had a series of jobs writing for newspapers. He soon started specializing in research articles about Canadian Indian tribes which included extended visits to the Blackfoot, Blood, and Sarcee "reserves." Along the way, he accumulated a lot of information about the customs and traditions of these Indians. He was also able to finagle an honorary tribal membership in the Blackfoot tribe and even a new name—Buffalo Child. He was quick to adopt and fully embrace his new name and new identity. His birthplace had moved half-way across the continent to Montana, and a whole new set of stories and explanations necessarily followed.

Long Lance moved to New York in 1927 and began working on his autobiography. *Long Lance* was published in August 1928 with considerable praise, and Long Lance's place as a celebrity was set. He was in great demand as a speaker and obviously had come to believe most of what was written in the clippings he meticulously put in his scrapbook. A true measure of his importance was that shortly after his autobiography was published, he was approached by the B.F. Goodrich Company to design and endorse a new running shoe. An ad in the April 1930 edition of *Boys' Life* proclaimed that Chief Long Lance himself had fashioned the prototype for the shoe using only a razor blade and a pair of old shoes. It went on to introduce him as a "Blackfoot Indian Chief. Born in a tepee. Trick rider for Buffalo Bill. Tackle on famous Carlisle football team. Captain in World War. Wounded, decorated for bravery. Light heavyweight boxing champion of Canadian army. As a wrestler he conquered the heavy-weight champion of the U.S. Army, 73 pounds heavier than he. In British Secret Service. Author of 'Long Lance.' Avid sportsman." And, for 10 cents you could order a copy of his pamphlet, "How to Speak in Indian Sign Language." Even his friend but mythical teammate, Jim Thorpe, endorsed the shoe.[8]

By 1930, Long Lance had started describing himself as an advocate for Indian rights, and he was certainly articulate and sincere. Despite that, it is unlikely that he and Chauncey knew each other very well, if at all, before the filming of *The Silent Enemy*. They simply moved in different circles. However, in an April 25, 1917, letter to General Pratt, Chauncey wrote that "there are some American Indians fighting in Europe with the allies. One of them is Sylvester Long Lance, a Carlisle graduate who is now in the British army as a lieutenant. Had it been not been for General

19. The Silent Enemy

Pratt found the old Carlisle School, Long Lance today would have remained on some reservation and never see the world."⁹ So, several years before they actually worked together and before Chauncey got to know Long Lance, he did not question his Indianness or his bravery.

Long Lance prepared a manuscript which attacked the Bureau of Indian Affairs—a position not unlike that of many legitimate Indian reformers of the time. His criticisms were valid. Unfortunately for Long Lance, his publisher had decided to send an advance copy of the autobiographical *Long Lance* to Charles Burke, the Commissioner of Indian Affairs. After investigating Long Lance's background, Burke replied that he considered it "readable" but "a publication of fiction."¹⁰ With the noose tightening, it was clearly time for Long Lance to escape. The movie deal seemed too good to pass up, and it was going to be filmed in northern Canada, hopefully away from prying eyes. By 1930, Long Lance found himself dangerously balanced on a precipice comprised of celebrity, legitimate concern for the well-being of Native Americans, fraudulency, and self-deception. It was inevitable that when put into a situation of daily contact with a person of integrity like Chauncey Yellow Robe, that balance would be irrevocably destroyed.

Sylvester Long was also known as Chief Buffalo Child Long Lance. He was also recognized as the "great imposter" who manufactured stories about his heritage and experience. He portrayed Baluk in *The Silent Enemy* (courtesy Glenbow Archives NA 1771-1).

Chauncey had expressed concerns about Long Lance from the beginning. For lack of a better explanation, he just did not seem Indian. He looked Indian, but that was not enough for Chauncey. He showed up for meals on time; he was loud and gregarious; his "war dances" were frenetic and uncontrolled; his use of sign language was inaccurate. After the film was complete, Chauncey made inquiries into Long Lance's authenticity—even to the point of contacting the Bureau of Indian Affairs directly. Long Lance was being critically acclaimed for his part in the movie. The reviews were fantastic, but when Long Lance finally met with Will Chanler, the film company's legal counsel, and was greeted by a cold, "Hello, Sylvester," he knew the charade was just about over.[11] He equivocated as best he could, but the rumors began to flow. After publicizing the movie as long as he comfortably could, his life spiraled downward. He started drinking excessively, and eventually killed himself with a shot from a .45 caliber pistol to his head on March 20, 1932.

Molly Spotted Elk, a Penobscot Indian who was a dancer and actress, portrayed Neewa in *The Silent Enemy* (courtesy Abbe Museum, Bar Harbor, Maine).

A beautiful young entertainer was chosen to play the role of Neewa, daughter of the chief and love interest of the noble Baluk and the tricky Dagwan. Burden had met Molly Spotted Elk as the Indian dancer at Texas Guinan's club in New York. Molly was born Mary Alice Nelson on Indian Island in Wabanaki country, a geographical area where Algonquin-speaking tribes lived, including the Penobscot. By November 17, 1903, Molly's birthday, most of the families lived in single-family homes, rather than tipis or wigwams. Molly had seven younger siblings. Eunice, her youngest sister, was the first Penobscot to earn a Ph.D.

There were several factors in Molly's early childhood that set her path for her years ahead. One, she worked hard

19. The Silent Enemy

from an early age and took pride in doing a good job at whatever she did. She cared for other people's children and scrubbed floors. As the oldest, she contributed to the income of the family from an early age, picking and selling berries and jam, weaving grass baskets. The hard work carried over into her schooling. At six she went to the island school and was taught by nuns. She loved to read and she treasured books, but she also liked to listen to the tribal elders telling stories. She committed them to memory and years later typed the legends in a collection and wrote an introduction to go with them. She described how Ach-zal-leek, would tell Molly a story in exchange for chopping wood for the kitchen stove. Another favorite was Hemlock Joe, an old man who was an invalid, but who told stories and acted out the parts with great drama and flourish. She continued to be active and earn her way all her life, and she continued her education of things both native and new to her. She wanted to become a writer and her interest in her own culture and history no doubt influenced her decisions to study ethnography and anthropology as an adult. She also studied French, which would serve her well in her European travels.

Two, Molly was a talented musician and dancer. She saved money to go to occasional movies or vaudeville shows, and she participated in dances on the island, especially in the summer tourist months. When she was nine, she traded housework for ballet lessons from a teacher in Bangor, 12 miles away. She studied piano and voice when she was younger and at 17 she went to Boston to get a job in a vaudeville show. This was not uncommon because by the 1920s Indians were popular and exotic entertainment. She was talented and she worked, sending money home to help her family and writing regular letters to tell them about her adventures. Apparently Molly was a tough critic on herself and always thought she could improve, even when critics lavished her with praise.

Three, Molly suffered from tuberculosis when she was young. She was petite and delicate, and her ill-health continued to plague her throughout her life. While filming in Canada, Molly kept a diary, documenting some of the hardships of the shoot, including frequent illnesses of the entire crew, and broken bones and aches and pains from strenuous scenes. She describes how they got their mail by dogsled, how they entertained themselves at night after putting in hard hours filming. She kept a rigorous exercise program to keep her strength and her dancer's figure, often hiking with Yellow Robe and Long Lance. She talked with Ilia Tolstoy about their common interest in anthropology and ethnography, and literature. The girl who was born on Indian Island, Maine, in 1903 was just beginning to participate in the world on a grand scale, which she had always dreamed of doing.

After the film's release, Molly returned to club dancing in New York, and in 1931 sailed for France as the American Indian representative in the ballet corps of the International Colonial Exposition. She performed in cabarets and recitals in Paris for royalty and artists and developed quite a following. One of the journalists who wrote about her was Jean Archambaud who was with the *Paris Soir* daily.[12] His name began to appear in Molly's diary. It wasn't long before she moved in with his parents, and though he asked her to marry him, she wanted to retain her independence. They traveled across Europe and Molly continued to put off returning home—and put off the idea of marriage. She joined the literary and political circles of Paris but missed her family and home, and in 1936 returned to her family in the U.S., pregnant, yet still unwilling to lose her identity through the institution of marriage.

She gave birth to Jean, Archambaud's daughter and in 1938 returned to France with her. The family enjoyed the city activities and visiting his parents outside Paris, but the political events of the day were threatening. Hitler's troops went into the Rhineland and after that they invaded Poland. Nazi troops occupied Paris and Molly felt she had to get out of the country with her daughter while Jean tried to get a visa. By cart, ambulance and by foot—with German planes overhead—she made her way to Spain where transportation was arranged to sail home. Though she and Jean exchanged letters after he surfaced in Vichy France, they were never to see each other again. He died in 1941 after a brief stay in the hospital. By all accounts, Molly was never the same again and, in fact, spent a year in a mental institution in Bangor, Maine. Molly died alone at the age of seventy-five. "Two weeks after her mother's death, she died of a fall."[13]

An interesting postscript to Molly Spotted Elk's story is that her lone grandson, John S. Moore, was involved in the American Indian Movement occupation of Wounded Knee in 1973. The next year he was found dead from multiple stab wounds on his face and in his throat at an A.I.M. "barracks" in Lincoln, Nebraska. What might appear to be a very suspicious death was ruled a suicide. The suicide ruling was changed to "unknown," but there was no further investigation.

Chief Akawansh, chief of the Golden Land Band of Ojibwas, played Dagwan the sinister medicine man. He had served as a guide for white

19. The Silent Enemy

people in the past, and his English name was Paul Benoit of Ontario. He just happened to be in the area when casting started. Dagwan is the romantic rival of Baluk for the affection of Chief Chetoga's daughter, Neewa. Unlike other principal characters from this film, his name does not appear in entertainment or political archives after his experience in the movie. Because the Indians in the movie were not professionals, much of their performances were fresh and uncontrived, making the action more authentic. For instance, George McDougal, or Cheeka, playing the young son of the old chief, thought that when Long Lance stood atop the funeral pyre he was really going to die. The film captured his genuine emotion and distress.

It is likely that animal rights groups would not be pleased with the handling of animal actors used in the film. The producers were reticent in discussing the manner in which the animal sequences were filmed, but the fundamental approach was to try to gather the animals in large, natural fenced in areas and then to take as much time as necessary to catch them being normal. Therefore, the filmmakers sometimes had to wait months to get just the right, natural looking shot. Other times, nature had to be helped. The fight between the bears and mountain lion over a dead deer carcass was enhanced by locking both species up for a prolonged period without food. The fight was real. The wolf versus moose scene and the subsequent Long Lance versus moose scene were both dangerous and graphic. One scene featured an angry bear chasing Neewa (Molly). The bear got extremely close and apparently jumped across a crevice it was not supposed to be able to negotiate. Molly said that she felt the hot breath of the bear closing on her.[14] Stories differ as to who killed the bear and how it was killed. Suffice it to say that it was not a well-placed arrow from Baluk, but more likely a well-placed bullet from Bob Miller who was hanging by a rope just out of camera range Not all nature scenes involved killing or abusing animals, and many were breath-taking and ground-breaking.

In 2012, another "lost" movie about and starring American Indians was discovered and restored. *The Daughter of Dawn* was an 80-minute, six-reel silent film with an all-Indian cast shot in July 1920 in Oklahoma on the Wichita Mountains Wildlife Refuge. "This wildly ambitious project had an all-Native cast, just one cameraman, no costumes, no lighting, no props, and wild buffalo."[15] It was not released at the time. This film's importance is demonstrated by the fact that the "Library of Congress in Washington, D.C. (has) selected 'The Daughter of Dawn,' as one of the films

Chauncey Yellow Robe

inducted to its 2013 National Film Registry, a collection of cinematic treasures that represent important cultural, artistic and historic achievements in filmmaking"[16] The authenticity that Chauncey insisted on is becoming the standard for depictions of Native Americans in film. The uproar about Johnny Depp playing Tonto in *The Lone Ranger* notwithstanding.

20

Latter Years

The last years of Chauncey's life were eventful and far from serene. First, his beloved wife died in April of 1927. Despite the fact that she had been extremely ill for years and died emaciated, Chauncey wrote to a friend that "she was in the prime of her life, a beautiful womanhood when she died."[1] Later that summer, Rosebud moved to New York City to pursue an acting career. Most fathers would feel much angst thinking about the possibilities inherent in that move. Chauncey's concerns were somewhat mitigated when a woman from Rosebud's university volunteered to accompany her as a chaperone. Rosebud told the story this way. "She'd said, 'I would like to go with you.' So, my father said, 'Well, if … if she goes with you … it will be alright.' I think I'm the only woman that ever went to Broadway with a chaperon because she was my chaperon. She wasn't a very good chaperon because I married the producer/director. And, uh, the, uhm … the upshot of it was that the understanding was that I would go for a year and then come back to the University of South Dakota, and I never did."[2]

Rosebud's chaperone had introduced her to the producer—Arthur de Cinq Mars (who was known professionally as Arthur Seymour). He was twenty-five years her senior. They were married within a year, and their daughter was born in 1929.

Rosebud admitted that she was probably the favored child. "I think he treated me more like a child beloved than he did Chaucina and Evelyn. And I—I think was a little spoiled."[3] As mentioned previously, Rosebud is the topic of a biography, *The Real Rosebud: The Triumph of a Lakota Woman*, written by Marjorie Weinberg. Her acting career and time she spent at the Indian Village at Jones Beach are well-chronicled in that work. However, Weinberg describes the book as a biography of the Yellow Robe family, but since the book was written essentially as an homage to Rosebud,

Chauncey Yellow Robe

a person she clearly loved and admired, and she might be excused for its omissions and inaccuracies about Chauncey in particular and the rest of the family in general. Mildred Fielder's *Sioux Indian Leaders* is another frequently cited book that deals with Chauncey. It too, unfortunately, is error ridden.

In May of 1928, his second oldest daughter, Chaucina married Louis A. Roubideaux in Hot Springs, South Dakota.[4] In her oral family history Rosebud said that "Chaucina, about that time then, uh, went back to the reservation. She stayed with my Aunt, uhm, Agnes. [Woman laughing in the background.] And, uh, my little sister then—my mother was dead, you know."[5] Whether the truth about what Chaucina was actually doing at about this time explains either Rosebud's stammering or the background laughter remains to be seen. Regardless, there is no doubt that the topic was off-limits to the family from that point on until the present. Mr. Roubideaux sued Chaucina for divorce while she was living in New York. It was granted on September 21, 1932.[6] The cause of action was given as "illegal marriage" probably referring to the question of her age at the time of the marriage. Depending on the date of birth, she was anywhere from fourteen to nineteen years old. To complicate things even more, the marriage record gives the date of their marriage as May 23, 1928, while the divorce decree lists it as May 23, 1929. Those members of the family who will talk about the marriage say that Chaucina was a victim of domestic violence. Chauncey could not have been pleased with either scenario.

The youngest daughter, Evelyn, spent the first years of her life in South Dakota, but relocated to New York after her mother died in 1927. Rosebud remembered that "then Evelyn came along, too.... And, uh, Evelyn was ... about six years old when my father died."[7] Chauncey had brought her to New York where she lived with Rosebud. By all accounts, Chauncey wanted to have a son. Rosebud said that "and, uh, he really wanted a son very badly. And, of course, I turned to be—turned out to be a girl."[8] Weinberg recounts that Chauncey was so certain his first child was going to be a boy that no girl's name had been chosen, but that he continued to hope "for a son to follow in his footsteps."[9] Some maintain that he did have a son.

The strange tale of Chauncey Yellow Robe, Jr., seems to have originated in a letter Clair F. Maynard wrote to Mildred Fielder in 1971. In that letter Mr. Maynard, who had been a teacher at the (Rapid City) Sioux Sanatorium Day School, said that

20. Latter Years

I have seen their son, Chauncey Yellow Robe, paint Black Hills scenes, at which he is very good. When I came to Rapid City during the early '40's, he would be painting like at Gambles, and would complete such a picture in twenty to thirty minutes, selling them for $4.00. But I understand he moved to Arizona where he was engaged in religious work as a lay reader a few years ago.[10]

Evidently that was all the proof Fielder needed. There is certainly no record of the birth of Chauncey, Jr., and Rosebud was adamant in her assertion that there was no such person. In a gently worded letter to Fielder in 1976, she said that "we are only sad that there are mistakes (in your book) which could have been easily remedied by the inclusion of additional material from the (Rapid City) *Journal*. As you can see from the enclosed Photostats, no son was listed among the heirs of my father, only three children as listed in his obituary."[11] Rosebud further pointed out that the mother was Swiss-German and not French Canadian as Fielder had said. Fielder acknowledged in her book that only the three daughters were named in the obituary.

Writing in 1977, Frederick J. Dockstader, said that "he [Chauncey] had married a French Canadian nurse, by whom he had four children—Evelyn, Rosebud, Chaucina, and Chauncey, Jr."[12] Not surprisingly, Fielder's book was listed as a reference for Dockstader's *Great North American Indian Leaders* in which the claim was made. In search for explanations for this mistake, there are several possibilities. First and simplest, Maynard was wrong. In my conversation with Maynard's son, he acknowledged that his father was probably just wrong. He had taught and met thousands of people over the course of his career, and he probably had confused things. Second, by that time, Chauncey Yellow Robe was probably not such an unusual name. Yellow Robes had become quite common on Rosebud and on other reservations, or Fielder and Dockstader simply did not check it out. Finally, by that time Chauncey was a widely recognized person. Someone might have just decided that it was in his best interest to be his son. All of these possibilities reinforce the problems with Native American research I have mentioned previously. Records are inconsistent; names are confusing; and oral recollections are not always accurate.

It was later in 1927 that Chauncey seemed to toy with the idea of running for Congress. In a story that appeared in *The Evening Sentinel* in Carlisle, it was reported that Chauncey, riding on the crest of his role in conferring the chiefdom of Calvin Coolidge, had been urged to become

Chauncey Yellow Robe

"the Democratic candidate to oppose William Williamson in the next campaign."[13] Chauncey did not squelch that rumor even though he had been living in New York with his daughter. In a letter to the *Hot Springs* (SD) *Star* He said, "I choose to run for congress from South Dakota in two years from now. My going to New York or any other cause should not bar my citizenship of South Dakota."[14] Additionally, he had retired from his civil service and was no longer prohibited from engaging in political activities. He died before he had the chance to realize his political ambitions. He officially resigned from his position at the Rapid City School on September 1, 1928. On August 8, 1928, he wrote to the Commissioner of Indian Affairs (through Superintendent Mote) "I hereby tender my resignation as Disciplinarian of the Rapid City Indian School, take effective—September 1st; in order to go into another field of activity. I regret to leave the Indian school service at this time in which I have served so long. Farewell with many thanks for all of the past favors."[15]

21

The Yellow Robe Daughters

As mentioned previously, while researching this book, one of Chauncey Yellow Robe's grandchildren wrote me a letter explaining that she would not be sending any pictures or discussing any information about the family. Furthermore she said that her aunt Evelyn (Chauncey's daughter) "feels there are enough books out there about Chauncey." Ironically, it is the almost total absence of accurate accounts about him that inspired me to write the book. Like many other important but relatively unknown Native Americans, Chauncey Yellow Robe deserves to have a thoroughly researched and objectively written biography about him. His life and his accomplishments can speak for themselves only if they are given a voice. An equally compelling case could be made for each his daughters. However, only Rosebud has been the subject of a published biography. In fact, that biography, *The Real Rosebud: The Triumph of a Lakota Woman* by Marjorie Weinberg, contains one of the few published accounts of Chauncey's life.

Weinberg relies on Rosebud's memories and papers, the publications of the Carlisle Indian Institute, and an elusive "unpublished" biography of Chauncey written by Ruth Brown. The objectivity of some of these sources is subject to question. Weinberg includes only superficial and limited information about Chauncey's other daughters—Chaucina and Evelyn. She even incorrectly gives the name of one of Chaucina's daughter, Fawn Stitman, as Fawn Sitman, giving further credence to the fact that the main focus of her work was Rosebud.[1]

Rosebud Yellow Robe was born on February 26, 1907, in Rapid City. The eldest of the three daughters, Chauncey likely named her after the Rosebud Reservation where she and her extended family were enrolled members. Despite the fact that her father worked at the Rapid City Indian School, Rosebud attended the public schools in Rapid City.

In 1925, she enrolled at the University of South Dakota in Vermillion. When she first set foot on campus, she was one of two Indians enrolled. She attracted much positive attention while there and performed traditional Indian dances as a contestant in the yearly Strollers performances. The Strollers staged musical and variety shows put on by students. Reportedly, she rushed a sorority only to be denied admission because the sorority's charter permitted only white members. Rosebud returned to Rapid City to help care for her gravely ill mother and did so until Lillian's death in April of 1927.

Shortly thereafter, events brought Rosebud national attention and admiration. Rosebud effectively stole the show when Chauncey took part in the "chiefing" of President Calvin Coolidge on August 4, 1927, at Deadwood. Her picture and, unfortunately, that of the war-bonneted president appeared in newspapers throughout the world. Rosebud soon moved to New York to pursue a career in entertainment.

In 1929, Rosebud married newspaper reporter and part-time theatrical manager/agent Arthur (de Cinq Mars) Seymour, although he was twenty-five years older than she. Their daughter, whom they named Tahcawin de Cinq-Mars Moy, was born that same year. Rosebud appeared at various nightclubs and hotels. Later her career expanded to include a radio show on CBS Radio. It was also during this time that her two sisters started living with her.

After Chauncey's death, Rosebud undertook what she came to see as her life's work. She began teaching young people about traditional Native American culture through the auspices of the Jones Beach Indian Village at Long Island, New York. She became the director of the village in 1930 and continued in that position for twenty years. Rosebud's first husband died in 1949, and two years later she married photographer Alfred A. Frantz. She died on October 5, 1992, and is buried near her father and mother in Rapid City.

Rosebud remains arguably the most well-known of the Yellow Robe daughters but only because of Weinberg's book. All three were notable and accomplished. Ironically, Rosebud's fame primarily came from being in entertainment or show business, writing, and speaking, and she certainly capitalized on her "Indianness."

Chaucina, the second daughter, has usually been referred to as "the

21. The Yellow Robe Daughters

strong one." Della Vik, a photographer and supposedly a friend of the Yellow Robes, indelicately described Chaucina as "more muscular and angular and by comparison to Rosebud was more uncouth in general."[2] Rosebud described her as "a tomboy." She might also be called the adventurous one, the athletic one, or the independent-minded one. It is interesting that the interviewer for Rosebud's oral history recording, Herbert Hoover (not the president), introduced Rosebud as "a sister ... of the very distinguished Chaucina White Horse, uh, who recommended originally and helped develop the Chicago Indian Oral History community."[3]

Chaucina's life was an interesting mixture of show business, a little hustle, and a lot of advocacy. Unfortunately, most of the things that are written about her only mention that she worked with the R.H. Donnelly Company selling ads for the Yellow Pages. She is included in the work *Women Building Chicago, 1790–1990*[4] and deserves much more. Rosebud said that "she was always the one who would go first. She was a leader."[5]

The responsibility of taking care of her mother during her extended illness fell primarily on Chaucina. Initially, Rosebud was away at school, and Evelyn was a young child. After her mother died and she had graduated from school, Chaucina took up residence on the Rosebud Reservation. Relatives living today say that she "ran away from home."

This was a significant move for several reasons. Chauncey's family was not particularly pleased that he had married a white woman and familial contact on the reservation was limited. Yellow Robe descendants on Rosebud still harbor some of those feelings. As mentioned previously, Chaucina soon married Louis A. Roubideaux in Hot Springs in 1928 (or 1929). Nothing is written about the next couple of years of her life except that she lived on the reservation. Hoover (Rosebud's interviewer) broached the topic of what Chaucina did after leaving Rapid City several times during the interview and generally got answers like this one: "Uhm ... she, you know, this may solve a problem about the, uh, about the tape. She married, uh, Lee White Horse."[6] She conveniently left out the reservation years. Rosebud said that she was a quick study and that "she knew more about Lakota [language] than she let on. Because she picked it up very rapidly."[7]

After moving (or being moved) to New York, Chaucina again demonstrated her independence. Despite the horrible financial crisis during the depression, she got a job as a salesperson at Macy's Department Store and was living independently. Always energetic and never complacent, in addition to working, she took a few college courses thinking about a legal career. Later she met and married Henry Ray Sutton (also known as Lee Whitehorse or White Horse). Mr. Whitehorse was an Arapaho from Oklahoma who was a singer and performer. Chaucina became the third Yellow Robe to have a "career" in show business. She often stood as the target while Lee shot arrows around her. Rosebud described their act this way.

> So, he went with, uh, uh ... the, uh, sportsmen shows. And, of course, she went along with him. And I don't know whether she ever told you about this. If anyone had courage, she had the most courage of any person I have—I would never let anyone do that! ... Because she would stand there ... and Crazy Bull told me about it.... I–I never saw it! He did. And he said he saw it one time when Lee missed. And it went right here in her hip. She just pulled the arrow out and walked off![8]

Chaucina was an active advocate for Indian rights and services—especially in urban areas. She worked tirelessly for better health care services as well as services for the elderly. She was one of 4,000 carefully chosen delegates to the 1971 White House Conference on Aging. The assembly tried to generate and sustain national interest in issues ranging from nutrition and health care to matters of religion and spirituality as they relate specifically to the aged. From that effort, she moved on to a leadership role in the creation of the National Indian Council on Aging.

Far from being a "snake oil" promoter as she is sometimes portrayed, Chaucina was an advocate for the holistic support of Indians—especially those who had relocated or who had been relocated to the city. She also worked as a job placement facilitator and counselor for young, unemployed Indians in the city. Her paper, "The Indians of Chicago: A Perspective,"[9] is regarded as a defining account of not only the deplorable conditions Indians experienced in urban areas but also why they might have chosen to move there.

She also felt that the individual stories and histories of the aged Indians, the Elders, living in Chicago, needed to be recorded and kept. One of her final acts of advocacy was her support of the Newberry Library Conference on Urban Indians and the Chicago American Indian Oral History Project which resulted in the audio taping of interviews that took place in 1983—after her death.

Chaucina's husband, Lee Whitehorse Sutton, also was responsible for preserving elements of the American Indian's way of life. Some forty

21. The Yellow Robe Daughters

songs that Lee had recorded were primarily traditional songs of tribes that live or lived in the Upper Plains and Oklahoma. These recordings serve not only as a record of traditional Indian music, but they also reflect the "diversity" that was present among the Indians living in mid–twentieth century Chicago. Chicago. Each song is accompanied by interpretations and explanations. This collection is housed at the Marquette University Library.

The youngest Yellow Robe daughter, Evelyn was born on December 25, 1919 (some sources give the date as 1920, and in a 1976 letter to Mildred Fielder, Rosebud said that she was born in 1921).[10] She moved to New York when she was around seven years old and was raised by her sister Rosebud. Like the other Yellow Robes, Evelyn's story is often inaccurately told. Della Vik said that "Evelyn, the youngest child, was much like Rosebud. She attended Carlyle [sic] as did her father."[11] Evelyn attended Flushing High School and graduated from Bayside High School in 1938. Like her sisters, Evelyn was intelligent, motivated, and ambitious. She graduated from the prestigious Mount Holyoke College in South Hadley, Massachusetts, in 1942. She distinguished herself there, graduating *magna cum laude* with concentrations in speech and psychology. Evelyn worked at Jones Beach State Park in New York alongside Rosebud and cultivated an interest in all things Indian, including crafts, storytelling, dancing, artifact collection, and even archery. After obtaining her BA at Mount Holyoke she received her MA and Ph.D. from Northwestern University in Chicago in speech pathology, Evelyn received a John Hay Fellowship, Ford Foundation Fellowship, and was the first Native American to be given a Fulbright Award. She began traveling, studying, and presenting abroad and earned an international reputation in her field. She taught at Northwestern, Mount Holyoke, and Vassar.

Like her sisters, her interest in Indian heritage and contemporary Indian issues grew and matured. Like her father and his mentor, Richard Pratt, she believed in the transformative power of education. In 1944, the *Mount Holyoke News* reported that

> Someday, Miss Yellow Robe hopes to establish a program through the Indian Office for the education of all Indians throughout the country. She is well aware of the weaknesses of the old system in which her own father suffered under when he went to the Carlisle Indian School.... Miss Yellow Robe prefers bringing schools to the reservation until such time as the Indians will have the knowledge and confidence to go out into the white man's world.[12]

Chauncey Yellow Robe

Chauncey would never suggest that he "suffered" at Carlisle. He flourished there; he worked his entire life at schools that took children from the reservations; and he championed both the school and its founder all of his life. However, it is interesting to juxtapose what Evelyn advocated and what Chauncey espoused at the Congress of Nations at the opening of the World's Columbian Exposition. In 1893, reformers advocated assimilation and saw off-reservation boarding schools as the best way to accomplish that and to "kill the Indian." By 1944, some reformers felt that reservation schools could equip Indians for life in the white man's world. Both groups thought that education was the key, and both thought that the Indian had actually to enter the white's man world to succeed. Evelyn's life work and considerable accomplishments had nothing to do with Indian education. Despite the fact that he died while she was very young, Evelyn's life connected with Chauncey's in other ways.

Like Chauncey, Evelyn was either unable or unwilling to disassociate with the Sitting Bull legacy. And like in her father's case, that association seemed to add an air of legitimacy and authenticity when it was needed most. Her appointment to a teaching position at Mount Holyoke was noted in the local newspaper. "Miss Evelyn Yellow Robe (she had stopped using just the name Robe) a Sioux Indian, and great grandniece of Sitting Bull, has been appointed a speech instructor at Mount Holyoke College it was announced today." When it was announced that she was receiving the 1946 Indian Achievement Medal from the Indian Council Fire, she was even identified as a "great granddaughter of Sitting Bull, Sioux chief and the victor of Custer's last stand."[13] The Sitting Bull connection was repeated in an announcement about Evelyn's appointment to a teaching position at Vassar College.

In December 1949, Evelyn was chosen to serve on the National Film Committee of the Association on Indian Affairs.[14] The purpose of the committee was to serve as an advisory, review, and research center for the film industry in an effort to more authentically represent Native Americans in movies. Chauncey's concern for authenticity in the representation of Indians had been largely responsible for his accepting the role in *The Silent Enemy*.

Evelyn is still best known in and around the Rosebud Reservation for a project she undertook in 1947. During the summer of that year, Evelyn returned to South Dakota and recorded the songs, performances, and stories performed by Indians on the Rosebud and Pine Ridge reservations.

21. The Yellow Robe Daughters

These recordings, along with some partial translations, are housed at the Folklife Center of the Library on Congress in Washington, D.C. They were donated by Rosebud. Some of the songs were apparently created on the spot as honorings to her and other members of the Yellow Robe family. One of the songs, titled "Song in Honor of Tasingai" (a reference to Chauncey's father), seems to some extent to sum up the Yellow Robe saga. The song was performed by Charles Red Breath Bear:

> My friends, you think that I am a white man.
> Some days I am Indian. Yellow Robe says so.
> Uncle Sam wants me to be white man
> but I love my Indian customs.[15]

Evelyn's attempt to capture and hopefully preserve some of the Indian ways was not universally appreciated. Relatives still on Rosebud point to the fact that she was a "half breed" and that "real Indians just do not do

The Yellow Robe daughters (from left) Evelyn, Rosebud, and Chaucina in 1980 (courtesy Rosebud Yellow Robe Frantz Collection, South Dakota Historical Society, H95-004).

those things." These same people suggest that most of the family simply refused to go along with her project and that many who did so did it in a mocking or tongue-in-cheek way. Regardless, Evelyn Yellow Robe's professional accomplishments and her efforts to improve the way Indians were represented in movies and other media earned her a nomination for inclusion on the website Native Village's list of most important Native Americans. She is the only Yellow Robe who was even nominated.

Dr. Evelyn Yellow Robe married Dr. Hans Finkbeiner in 1959 at the Church-in-the-Gardens in Forest Hills, New York. They moved to Germany, and she gained an international reputation in the area of speech pathology—and more specifically in the area of laryngeal physiology. She died in October 2016.

The accomplishments of the three Yellow Robe daughters were many and varied. However, one thing was abundantly clear. Chauncey's daughters did not lack confidence and did go out into the white man's world and succeeded there.

22

Chauncey's Death

My Brothers and friends, let us console ourselves with these brief words of understanding and comfort:
Thus saith the Lord: Refrain thy voice from weeping and thine eyes from tears, for the work shall find its reward, and there is hope for thy latter end...
Blessed is the man whose strength is in Thee, in whose heart are the highways to Thy will. Passing through the valley of weeping, they turn to a fountain of strength. Yes, into a rain shower abundant with blessing. Thus they go on from strength to strength, until each appeareth before Thee in Zion...
They shall come with mourning, but I will lead them with tender mercy. I will turn their weeping into joy. I will comfort them and make them rejoice after their sorrow...
My brothers and friends, in keeping with a custom of Free and Accepted Masons, we are united in this moment of sorrow to bid farewell to our Brother Chauncey.
It is well that we pause to ask God's blessings upon us, for only in Him can we find strength and hope. Let us pray...
Almighty God, grant us Thy blessing as we meet on this solemn occasion. Help us to look beyond the sadness of this moment to the light and hope of tomorrow. Thou knowest we are weak and unable to stand alone. Fill us then with the power and comfort of Thy presence, that we may say with assurance, as did Job of old in his grief, "The Lord gave, and the Lord hath taken away, blessed be the name of the Lord." Amen
Our Brother became a Free and Accepted Mason on April 23, 1915, in Rapid City Lodge No. 25.
He left our earthly family to unite with the heavenly family on April 6, 1930.
While we mourn his loss from our fraternal fellowship, we rejoice that we are citizens of two worlds. He has preceded us and has joined our host of Brethren in that other world where God, who is the Father and Master of us all, awaits his coming.
Always when we stand in the presence of death, we are tempted to ask the question, as did the prophet of old: "If a man die, shall he live again?" How empty our lives would be if there was no answer to this question! But God in His infinite mercy has given us the greatest gift of all—the promise to dwell in our

Chauncey Yellow Robe

hearts when we diligently seek Him. And, from that depth within each of us, we have always found the faith that sustains us even in the darkest and most difficult moments. So we can say with certainty that just as surely as the questions of fear and doubt arise in our minds, so comes the assurance that life does not end with death.

Our Masonic belief bears testimony:

That Man is a citizen of two worlds;

That only eternity can fulfill the dreams and hopes and ideals within each of us;

That a lifetime on earth is not enough;

That God in His infinite wisdom has plans that could not end in death.

That faith sustains us and helps dispel the fears that surround death.

Because our Brother Chauncey was a Mason, we know that this was his belief—the Immortality of the Soul was part of his spiritual vocabulary. He walked and worked and lived against the background of eternity. He believed that the God who created him and sustained him in life would not abandon him in death.

This white Apron is known as the Lambskin.

It is the badge of a Mason. Its whiteness served to remind our departed Brother of the innocence and purity of a righteous life. It reminds us that our Brother's earthly labors are finished. He has laid aside the working tools of life. May the record of our lives and actions be as pure and spotless as this fair emblem which will now be placed on the coffin of our departed Brother.

This sprig of Acacia is the emblem of our faith in the immortality of the Soul.

The evergreen leaves are symbolic of the conviction that life will continue to flourish even after death and that one day we shall be united in the house of many mansions, eternal in the heavens. This sprig of Acacia will now be placed on the coffin of our departed brother.

To you, the immediate family, relatives and friends of our departed Brother, we extend our deepest sympathy. We cannot fill the emptiness in your hearts. We can only urge that you turn to God, who alone can give you the strength to sustain you in this hour.

Believe that "there is a land of pure delight where saints immortal reign," and sing with the Psalmist:

"Yea, though I walk through the valley of the shadow of death, I will fear no evil.... Surely goodness and mercy shall follow me all the days of my life and I will dwell in the house of the Lord forever."

May god grant you peace and keep you under HIS WING.

There is no Death. What we call Death is but a sudden change; because we know not where it leads. Therefore it doth seem strange.

There is no Death. What we call Death is but a lasting sleep. They wake not soon who slumber so. Therefore we mourn ... we weep.

There is no Death. What we call Death is but surcease from strife. They do not die who we call dead. They go from life ... to Life.

We consign his body to the earth.

22. Chauncey's Death

We cherish his memory here.
We commend his spirit to God who gave it.[1]

With words like these from the Grand Master, Chauncey Yellow Robe was laid to rest in the Mountain View Cemetery in Rapid City. He died on the third anniversary of his wife's death, April 6, 1930. His death did not go unnoticed. Princess Atalie Unkalunt Rider, a multitalented Indian singer, poet, and activist praised Chauncey in interviews after his death. Newspapers like the *New York Times* carried his obituary. Ironically this obituary, which was carried verbatim by the Carlisle School newspaper, contained several errors that Marjorie Weinberg "corrected" later.

> Chief Chauncey Kills in the Bush Yellow Robe, a full-blooded Sioux Indian who spent his mature life in substituting education for the tomahawk of his forefathers and was a tribal brother of former President Coolidge, is dead. Chief Yellow Robe, as he was more commonly known, died of pneumonia on Sunday night in the Rockefeller Institute Hospital, York Avenue and Sixty-eighth Street, ending a picturesque and notable career. He was born on the Rosebud Indian Reservation 63 years ago.[2]

The obituary went on to say that the "chief" was generally recognized as one of the best educated Indians in the United States. There was no question about Chauncey's intelligence, but many other American Indians of the period were much better educated. Chauncey's friend Princess Atalie told the newspaper that he had planned to run for Congress as a Republican in South Dakota. The article reported that Chauncey had been born prior to the "Custer Massacre" and that his mother's brothers had taken part in it. His "chiefing" of Coolidge was mentioned as well as his years of service in Indian Service schools. It was also pointed out that Chauncey had married a white woman and had three daughters.

Weinberg's "corrections" included the following:

> There are many errors in the obit. I've corrected the following:
> Kills-in the Wood, or Timber------not Kills in the Bush
> Chauncey may have been much older that 63 at the time of his death. He said he was 15 years old when he arrived at Carlisle. His birthdate has varied by as much as 7 years. It was in August of 1927, that he presided at the Coolidge ceremony, recognizing Coolidge's administration for finally making American Indians citizens in 1924. Chaucina, not Chauncine.[3]

Perhaps the mistakes were understandable rather than ironic. So much of the account of Chauncey's life was exaggerated, hearsay, undocumented, or unsubstantiated. Even his hometown newspaper engaged in such hyperbole. In the *Rapid City Daily Journal*, it is repeated that "Mr. Robe was widely known as one of the best educated Indians in the United States."[4] It is interesting to note that both obituaries called him one of the best educated (full-blooded) Indians in the United States, but neither made reference to his Sitting Bull connection. His relationship to Sitting Bull might be legitimate. The claim that he was one of the best educated Indians certainly is not. As mentioned previously, his formal education did not go beyond the Carlisle Indian School. Hundreds of Indian children attended Carlisle.

Calvin Coolidge said of Chauncey, "He represented a trained and intelligent contact between two different races. He was a born leader who realized that the destiny of the Indian is indissolubly bound up with the destiny of our country. His loyalty to his tribe and his people made him a most patriotic American."[5] He was laid to rest next to Lillian in the cemetery. In 1992, Rosebud was buried next to them, and her husband, Arthur Frantz, was buried there in 1993.

23

Yellow Robes

As I researched the life of Chauncey Yellow Robe, I had the good fortune to be able to interview his lone surviving daughter and a granddaughter. I also interviewed Yellow Robes living in South Dakota, Montana, Arizona, New Mexico, and Washington. Some were relatives and knew it. Some had never heard of Chauncey. In one case, we were able to establish a connection if not a relationship. This Yellow Robe's uncle had been a policeman on the Rosebud reservation.

It is important to remember that Chauncey and his immediate family were not the only Yellow Robes. He had numerous brothers and sisters. The exact number is in dispute as is the exact number of wives Tasinag had in his lifetime. For purposes of description and comparison, it would be fairly convenient to say that the Yellow Robe family, after Tasinag, could be divided into two distinct divisions—Chauncey's family (Chauncey, Lillian, Rosebud, Chaucina, and Evelyn) and all the others. Such a division is both inaccurate and simplistic. Although Weinburg and others fail to mention the "other Yellow Robes," they married, they had children, they went to school, they had jobs, they achieved, they failed, and they have stories as well. They went to schools like Upper Cut Meat, the various boarding schools, Saint Francis, and Sinte Gleska University, not Northwestern or Holyoke. Some left the reservation, and some have not to this day. At least one traveled the world with Buffalo Bill Cody.

Several living relatives find it interesting that their fathers, grandfathers, and uncles were never considered or referred to as "hereditary chief" and did not consider themselves as such. More than one consider Chauncey's family as *iyeska*, or tainted with mixed blood, and resent the fact that they have garnered so much attention and respect. Several take pride in him and his family and have collected articles and pictures featuring them. Several have been gracious and forthcoming—willing to share stories;

others have been reluctant or even recalcitrant—not wanting to share much, if anything, with someone they did not know. Some have even said that another writer about the family had encouraged them not to talk with me. Those who were willing and anxious to talk provided interesting, provocative, and valuable information—much of it falling into that unwritten, or oral, category I mentioned. I have decided to focus on two. One lives on Rosebud, and one does not.

The pursuit of information about these other Yellow Robes led me to the Rosebud Reservation in South Dakota to meet and talk with Patti Romero. My first trip to Mission, South Dakota, took place on a hot day in June. My first contact there was when a young Indian man came up to me at the gas pump and asked me how things were in Rapid City. I was not the only, or even the whitest person, at the store; so I was a little taken aback by his question. Apparently from his tone of voice, being from Rapid was not necessarily a good thing. So when I responded, "It's still there," he replied, "Too bad." He explained that South Dakota was one of the states that had a numbering system for license plates that indicated which county your car was registered in and that the numbering was by population. My rental car tag began with a 2, so he knew that I was from Rapid City (Pennington County). He went on to say that the real purpose of the system was to give law enforcement officials the advantage of being able to see which cars were from the rez—the number 65 was from Shannon County (Pine Ridge) and the Todd County (Rosebud reservation) number was 67. Afterward, I called Patti and we met at the snack shop in the Buche's Foods store.

For many of the Yellow Robes, Patti, who still lives on the Rosebud reservation is seen as the unofficial family historian. Others in the family claim not to know who she is or what claim to relationship she actually has. Interestingly, other writers claim never to have met or talked with Patti. Patti is understandably confused and indignant about these claims and can recall specific dates, times, and places where she has met the very people who deny knowing her. Patti said, "Marjorie's [Weinberg] book messed up what took me a lifetime to compile.... I read Marjorie's book two or three times and tried to make sense of it but couldn't. I went over what I believe and yes, it made more sense. I will never allow someone who has not lived on the reservation and is not Indian to sway my thinking again. I had so much respect for my aunt Rosebud, I wanted to believe Marjorie's book."

23. Yellow Robes

Patti has specific ideas about people and events in the Yellow Robe family saga. For example, regarding how the Yellow Robe name came into being, she said that "before my uncle died he told me that his father told the story about the Yellow Robes. Our great-grandfather Yellow Robe was a Crow Indian. A band of Sioux was fighting a band of Crows. The Sioux defeated the Crow, but one Crow ran with his son. The Sioux surrounded him. The Crow told the Sioux whichever of you kill me I want you to take my son and raise him as your own, but I want him to keep his name Yellow Robe. A Sioux named Little Thunder killed him and brought him back to the Parmelee area [Lower Cut Meat]. When you read Marjorie's book Chauncey was born in Montana. My uncle was in the service with a Calvin Yellow Robe who was from the Crow Agency. He worked as a BIA policeman here in Rosebud." A Yellow Robe living in Havre, Montana, indicated that Calvin was his uncle.

Patti supports the family connection to Sitting Bull. In fact, she expands it. She said,

> I have a picture of Sitting Bull's daughter who is a dead ringer for one of my granddaughters. Pictures don't lie. A lot of people come to my house and a few look at her picture and tell me that little girl looks just like you when you were little. My own daughter looks at the picture and says "Gee, Mom, she sure looks like us." Oral history is that Yellow Robe was married to 3 of Sitting Bull's nieces. One could have been his daughter. Sitting Bull had children from Canada to Oklahoma. So, you can doubt what I say because it isn't written.... So, **MY** great grandmother could be Sitting Bull's daughter. Put that in your book. Again, you will have to remember that in our culture we do not dissect our relationships as Marjorie did when we talked on the phone."

Patti had previously indicated that Marjorie Weinberg had been insistent about saying that Patti's grandfather was "only" a half-brother to Chauncey.

Patti is an unrestrained, uncensored person who possesses an amazing and apparently limitless amount of information about all branches of the Yellow Robe family tree. She is the daughter of Angeline Yellow Robe. Angeline was the daughter of Joe Yellow Robe (II). Patti explained that the first Joseph Yellow Robe had died and that her grandfather was given his name when he was born. She "respectfully declined" to be recorded, saying that she did not feel comfortable revealing that much of herself. She then proceeded to recite more information about the Yellow Robe lineage than the census records reveal. She finally became so impatient and irritated with my attempts to take notes that she took my pen and pad, and in her nearly perfect handwriting, recorded the information herself. She wrote and diagrammed her way through countless generations of Yellow Robes without missing a beat. Interspersed in her account were recollections and reflections that revealed as much about her as they did the people she was discussing.

She talked introspectively about a time when she and her Uncle Tony were visiting in the Rosebud Creek area of Montana. She said that for some reason she felt almost a magnetic attraction to the region that she could not explain. She even asked if maybe she had been there before; she had not. Tony explained that this was the region the family had lived in at the time of Chauncey's birth before relocating to the reservation.

She talked at length about her grandfather being a horse whisperer long before the book or movie introduced the term. According to Patti, Joe was often the last resort for people who had tried everyone and everything else to train their horse. The famous rodeo star and actor Casey Tibbs, who was from the area, relied on Joe to train his horses. She also talked about her Uncle Christopher, who Patti said was called by television game show host Bob Barker the best basketball player he had ever seen. Barker lived on the Rosebud Reservation as a young man while his mother worked there. Despite the fact that he was barely five feet tall, Christopher could humble, defend, and outscore opponents who were much taller.

Patti is an outspoken advocate of the actual traditional Lakota lifestyle and values it. She sees the accumulated impact of the historical treatment of Indians as resulting in an inordinate number of cases involving alcoholism, drug abuse, mental illness, and sexual abuse among the native population. By way of example, she openly recounted her personal experiences and commented that her years of emotional emptiness were now long behind her. She said that the curiosity she had as a child and that she continues to have as an adult about her family and who she was has given her both strength and direction—something she hopes others in the family can find. Patti suggested that I visit the family cemetery at White Lake. After a great deal of driving around and more than a few stops for directions, I found it. According to Patti, Chauncey's father, and many other relatives were buried there among the brush, the briars, and barbed wire.

Theresa Nelson is the daughter of Ethel Yellow Robe who was the daughter of William—Chauncey's brother. Like Patti, Theresa thinks that the accomplishments of the entire family need to be acknowledged and

23. Yellow Robes

honored. Also like Patti, she is concerned about the lack of direction that seems evident to her in American Indians on and off the reservation. Theresa told me that every generation needs to try to make the life of the next generation measurably better than its own. Reservation life does not always make that easy. She related a story that she thought was uniquely symbolic for her family and Native Americans in general. According to Theresa, her grandfather was a mailman who actually witnessed the Wounded Knee Massacre from a nearby hill while he was on his route. He watched the government that was responsible for his livelihood murder essentially defenseless Indians—possibly even relatives. The irony was inescapable for Allison. She described how her grandfather, a peaceful man, cried as he told her about the massacre and how helpless he felt as he watched. She also described the helplessness that she has felt as an "aunt or grandmother" as young people—not just those who are blood kin—make bad decision after bad decision. She thinks that a knowledge and respect for the traditions and ways of the past would provide much needed direction. That is what the name Yellow Robe means to her, and she was not referring to Chauncey or his family. She was talking about William, Joseph, and the Yellow Robes who stayed.

Fast-forward to the present. Government commodities and payments had resulted in the loss of initiative and personal accountability for many Native Americans. Federal and state mandates that govern education and their emphasis on test scores have forced many Indian schools to discontinue courses in language and traditions. This cultural massacre started at the boarding schools continues today. Theresa's daughter has an excellent job with the federal government in public affairs, but she continues the oral tradition of storytelling, participates in powwows, and is a native speaker. She even adopted the Yellow Robe name in 2011 as a way of maintaining a connection with the past. Both mother and daughter talk with pride about their family; both are obviously proud of their heritage. However, they are estranged and never speak to each other. The family ties that interest them and connect them with the past do not connect them to each other.

Theresa, or "Bear Walks Close to Village," died of complications from diabetes on July 9, 2017. Like too many other Native Americans, much of her life in recent years was spent in hospitals and on dialysis. She was graceful and faithful throughout it all. She was described as being creative, intelligent, musical, athletic, and as a kind, loving soul. She was a Yellow

Chauncey Yellow Robe

Robe. I spoke with Theresa often during the preparation of this book and regret that she was unable to read it.

The Yellow Robe family cemetery sits atop a small but discernible rise in the southern South Dakota countryside. From the cemetery, you can see White Lake, the outline of a dirt road, and a few farms or ranches. It is quiet with only an occasional barking dog breaking the silence. Both in the morning and at sunset, vibrant colors dance across the respective horizons, and you are at least temporarily unaware or unconcerned with the fact that just a few miles away the electric colors of gambling machines lighten up the interior of the Rosebud Casino. Looking at the cemetery itself evokes a strikingly different feeling. Few headstones remain intact. Most are broken and unreadable. Weeds and briars make it hard to walk around. Yellow Robe, Search the Enemy, and William are some of the names that can be read. No one seems to care. Consider now the well-manicured grounds of the Mountain View Cemetery in Rapid City. Chauncey, Lillian, Rosebud and Alfred Frantz are buried there.

24

The Yellow Robe Name

This narrative began with what might have seemed to be an improbable linkage between Sarah Mather and Chauncey Yellow Robe family. She was from New England. He was from Indian Country. Her family and family name went back generations. His family name barely went back one generation. She was well-education and graduated from the prestigious Mount Holyoke College. He did not have any formal education before or after he went to Carlisle.

It does not require any great effort or contrivance to see why that connection makes sense. Both Sarah Mather and Chauncey Yellow Robe were associated with, and disciples of, Richard Pratt. Sarah Mather taught for him in Indian schools. Chauncey defied extraordinary odds and conventional wisdom by succeeding, enjoying, and even flourishing at Carlisle. His education there was a springboard for a career he pursued for most of his adult life working in off-reservation Indian boarding schools. Of Pratt, Chauncey said, "During my school days in Carlisle I was under the fatherly care of General R.H. Pratt…. Today I owe him all that I am."[1] Both were intelligent and articulate. Both had keen and self-deprecating senses of humor.

Once while working with Pratt's Florida Boys at Fort Marion, Mather grew frustrated trying to teach White Horse how to pronounce the word "teeth." In desperation, she removed her complete set (upper and lower) of false teeth in an attempt to give the Indian something to association with the word. Horrified, White Horse exclaimed, "Miss Mather no good!"[2] The class erupted so much that Pratt rushed in to see what was wrong.

Once while Chauncey was in Chicago at the World's Fair, a white woman approached him and asked why his face was not painted, despite the fact that he was dressed in his full Plains Indian regalia. Chauncey thoughtfully took measure of the situation and the woman. He asked for

The cemetery marker for "Lily" and Chauncey Yellow Robe is in Mountain View Cemetery in Rapid City (author's photograph).

her make-up kit and mirror. After applying the "war paint," Chauncey wryly responded, "You are right, paint makes the Indian—now I am a real one."[3]

On a more serious note, Both Yellow Robe and Mather believed that the future for the American Indian lay in assimilation. They both took that arduous journey between South Dakota and Carlisle, Pennsylvania. Mather traversed from Carlisle to South Dakota and back. Chauncey traveled from South Dakota to Carlisle and back. Both had non-conventional relationships that most of society did not condone. Mather had a female life partner. Chauncey married a white woman. Both had professional lives associated with teaching and education.

However, the tightest link is that they both became blessed and cursed with being part of famous families with immediately recognizable names, and both decided that it was important for them to break away from the locations where those names meant something. Sarah Mather left New England to teach people who previously had been among the untaught. Chauncey Yellow Robe decided that it was easier and more productive to be an Indian in white society than it was on the reservation.

24. The Yellow Robe Name

Broken headstones and waist-high weeds mar the Yellow Robe family cemetery outside Mission, Rosebud Indian Reservation, South Dakota (author's photograph).

Today, there are Yellow Robes of different tribal affiliations in states ranging from Pennsylvania to Washington. They are playwrights, musicians, law enforcement officers, actors, artisans, alcoholics, liquor store owners, homeless people, entrepreneurs, criminals, and victims of criminals. Both the 1990 and 2000 U.S. Census reports show that there were fewer than 100 people with the exact Yellow Robe surname in those years. The most productive internet search provided the unduplicated names of 82 Yellow Robes in 2012. They live or have lived in 19 states with the largest number still being in Montana and South Dakota. Without large scale DNA testing, it is impossible to say if these are related to Chauncey. Whether these Yellow Robes even know anything about Chauncey and his accomplishments is unknown, but one relative admitted to me that she was going to start using the name because it would help her business. The Yellow Robe name means something.

Chapter Notes

Preface

1. *Report of the Commissioner of Indian Affairs to the Secretary of the Interior for the Year 1871.* Washington, D.C.: Government Printing Office, 1872. 101.
2. "Native American (American Indian) GoodReads Members Discussion." Native American (American Indian) GoodReads Members. Accessed June 30, 2015.
3. Weinberg, Marjorie. *The Real Rosebud: The Triumph of a Lakota Woman.* Lincoln: University of Nebraska Press, 2004. i.
4. Wilson, Angela C. "American Indian History or Non-Indian Perceptions of American Indian History." *American Indian Quarterly* (Winter 1996): 3.

"Chauncey Yellow Robe"

1. Clark, Badger. "Chauncey Yellow Robe." *Pasque Petals* V, no. 2 (1930): 18.

Chapter 1

1. Erdoes, Richard, and Alphonso Ortiz. *Native American Myths and Legends.* New York: Pantheon, 1984. Recorded by Erdoes in 1969.
2. Yellow Robe, Chauncey. "My Boyhood Days." *The American Indian Magazine* IV, no. 1 (1916): 50–53.

Chapter 2

1. Telegram from Sarah Mather to William Pratt. September 29, 1878. Richard Henry Pratt Papers. Yale Collection of Western Americana, Beinecke Rare Book and Manuscript Library. Box 6, Folder 195.
2. Pratt, Richard Henry. *Battlefield and Classroom: Four Decades with the American Indian, 1867–1904.* New Haven: Yale University Press, 1964. 221.
3. *Ibid.*, 223.

Chapter 3

1. Yellow Robe, Richard. "An Indian Boy's Experience." *The Indian Helper* III, no. 17 (December 2, 1887).
2. Yellow Robe, Chauncey. "My Boyhood Days." *The American Indian Magazine* IV, no. 1 (1916): 50–53.
3. *Ibid.*
4. Yellow Robe, Richard. "An Indian Boy's Experience." 1.
5. Yellow Robe, Chauncey. "My Boyhood Days."

Chapter 4

1. Yellow Robe, Chauncey. "My Boyhood Days." *The American Indian Magazine* IV, no. 1 (1916): 50–53.
2. *Ibid.*
3. Adams, David Wallace. *Education for Extinction: American Indians and the Boarding School Experience, 1875–1928.* Lawrence: University Press of Kansas, 1995. 100.
4. Letter from Commissioner of Indian Affairs William A. Jones to Superintendent, Round Valley, California. January 11, 1902.

National Archives, Records of the Bureau of Indian Affairs.
 5. Terry, Frank. "Naming the Indians." *American Monthly Review of Reviews* 15 (March 1897): 301–307.
 6. Curiel, James. "Indigenous Resistance and Persistence." *Wicazo Sa Review*, 215–23.
 7. Bear, Luther. *My People, the Sioux*. Lincoln: University of Nebraska Press, 1975. 10.
 8. Oneroad, Amos E., and Alanson B. Skinner. *Being Dakota: Tales and Traditions of the Sisseton and Wahpeton*. Edited by Laura L. Anderson. St. Paul: Minnesota Historical Society Press, 2003. 89.
 9. Yellow Robe, Chauncey. "My Boyhood Days."

Chapter 5

 1. Official Report of the Nineteenth Annual Conference of Charities and Correction (1892), 46–59. Reprinted in Richard H. Pratt, *The Advantages of Mingling Indians with Whites: Americanizing the American Indians: Writings by the "Friends of the Indian," 1880–1900*. Cambridge, Mass.: Harvard University Press, 1973. 260–271.
 2. Pratt, Richard Henry. *The Indian Industrial School: Its Origin, Purposes and Difficulties Surmounted*. Carlisle, Pennsylvania: Hamilton Library Association, 1908. 42.
 3. Pratt, Richard Henry. *Battlefield and Classroom: Four Decades with the American Indian, 1867–1904*. New Haven: Yale University Press, 1964. 283.
 4. Coleman, Michael C. *American Indian Children at School, 1850–1930*. Jackson: University Press of Mississippi, 1993. 43.
 5. Adams, David Wallace. *Education for Extinction: American Indians and the Boarding School Experience, 1875–1928*. Lawrence: University Press of Kansas, 1995. 157.
 6. *Report of the Commissioner of Indian Affairs to the Secretary of the Interior for the Year 1871*. Washington, D.C.: Government Printing Office, 1887. xvii–xviii.
 7. Coleman, Michael C. *American Indian Children at School, 1850–1930*. 87.

 8. Segal, Jacqueline. *White Man's Club: Schools, Race, and the Struggle of Indian Acculturation*. Lincoln: University of Nebraska Press, 2007. 223–224.
 9. "Part IV—Academic Courses." In *Catalogue: United States Indian School*. Carlisle, Pennsylvania: Carlisle Indian School, 1912. 35.
 10. *Ibid.*, 37.
 11. Part II—The Carlisle Indian School Purpose. In *Catalogue: United States Indian School*. Carlisle, Pennsylvania: Carlisle Indian School, 1912. 10.
 12. Weinberg, Marjorie. *The Real Rosebud: The Triumph of a Lakota Woman*. Lincoln: University of Nebraska Press, 2004. 19.
 13. Segal, Jacqueline. *White Man's Club*. 168.
 14. Coleman, Michael C. *American Indian Children at School, 1850–1930*. 43.
 15. Textual Records of the Department of Interior, Office of Indian Affairs, Carlisle Indian School, Record Group 75. 2163492. Registry of Outings, 1881–1918.
 16. *The Indian Helper*, November 21, 1890.
 17. Moses, L. G. *Wild West Shows and the Images of American Indians, 1883–1933*. Albuquerque: University of New Mexico Press, 1999. 73–74.
 18. "Don't Agree with Them." *Wheeling Register*, June 16, 1890.
 19. "Buffalo Bill's Wild West Indians." *Washington Post*, August 5, 1890.
 20. "Painted Horse." *Aberdeen Daily News*, November 11, 1890.
 21. *Report of the Commissioner of Indian Affairs to the Secretary of the Interior for the Year 1892*. Washington, D.C.: Government Printing Office, 1892. 830
 22. *The Indian Helper* VIII, no. 6 (October 21, 1892).
 23. The Indian Census Rolls, 1885–1940 (National Archives Microfilm Publication M595).
 24. *Report of the Commissioner of Indian Affairs to the Secretary of the Interior for the Year 1892*. 830.
 25. U.S. Army, Register of Enlistments, 1798–1914. National Archives Publication

M233. Records of the Adjutant General's Office. Record Group 94.

Chapter 6

1. Robe, Rosebud, and Jerry Pinkney. *Tonweya and the Eagles: And Other Lakota Indian Tales*. New York: Dial, 1979. 15
2. "Grover Cleveland, Second Inaugural Address—March 4, 1893." Wikipedia. Accessed July 16, 2015.
3. *The Indian Helper* VIII, no. 6 (October 21, 1892). 2.
4. Pratt, Richard Henry. *Battlefield and Classroom: Four Decades with the American Indian, 1867–1904*. New Haven: Yale University Press, 1964. 307.
5. *Ibid.*, 303.
6. Segal, Jacqueline. *White Man's Club Schools: Race, and the Struggle of Indian Acculturation*. Lincoln: University of Nebraska Press, 2007. 46. "Miss Sickles Makes Charges; Tells Why There Are No Civilized Indians at the Fair." New York Times, October 8, 1893. Nytimes.com. Accessed July 16, 2015.
7. *The Indian Helper*. July 21, 1893.
8. *The Indian Helper*. August 11, 1893.
9. Yellow Robe, Chauncey. "The World's Fair Seen by an Aborigine." *The Red Man*, February 1, 1895.
10. *The Indian Helper*. March 27, 1891.
11. *The Indian Helper*. December 4, 1891.
12. Adams, David Wallace. *Education for Extinction: American Indians and the Boarding School Experience, 1875–1928*. Lawrence: University Press of Kansas, 1995. 23.

Chapter 7

1. Segal, Jacqueline. *White Man's Club: Schools, Race, and the Struggle of Indian Acculturation*. Lincoln: University of Nebraska Press, 2007. 159.
2. Adams, David Wallace. *Education for Extinction: American Indians and the Boarding School Experience, 1875–1928*. Lawrence: University Press of Kansas, 1995. 97.
3. Coleman, Michael C. *American Indian Children at School, 1850–1930*. Jackson: University Press of Mississippi, 1993. 43.
4. Treuer, David. *Rez Life: An Indian's Journey through Reservation Life*. New York: Atlantic Monthly, 2012. 270.
5. Ahern, Wilbert H. "An Experiment Aborted: Returned Indian Students in the Indian School Service, 1881–1908." *Ethnohistory* 44, no. 2. (Spring 1997): 263–264.
6. Trafzer, Clifford E., Jean A. Keller, and Lorene Sisquoc, eds. *Boarding School Blues: Revisiting American Indian Educational Experiences*. Lincoln: University of Nebraska Press, 2006. 43.
7. "Record of Living Graduates." In *Catalogue: United States Indian School*, 84–85. Carlisle, Pennsylvania: Carlisle Indian School, 1912.

Chapter 8

1. "A Demented Indian." *Atlanta Constitution*, November 30, 1895.
2. Perdue, Theda. *Race and the Atlanta Cotton States Exposition of 1895*. Athens: University of Georgia Press, 2010. 83.
3. *Report of the Commissioner of Indian Affairs to the Secretary of the Interior for the Year 1895*. Washington, D.C.: Government Printing Office, 1892. 55
4. *Atlanta Constitution*, September 20, 1895.
5. "A Demented Indian." *Atlanta Constitution*.
6. Weinberg, Marjorie. *The Real Rosebud: The Triumph of a Lakota Woman*. Lincoln: University of Nebraska Press, 2004. 7.
7. Indian Census Rolls, 1885–1940. National Archives Microfilm Publication. 1965. Microcopy 595.
8. Weinberg, Marjorie. *The Real Rosebud*. 7.
9. *The Official Catalogue of the Cotton States and International Exposition*. Atlanta: Chaflin and Mellichamp, 1895. 215.

Chapter 9

1. *Report of the Commissioner of Indian Affairs to the Secretary of the Interior for the Year 1895*. Washington, D.C.: Government Printing Office, 1892. 301
2. *Report of the Commissioner of Indian*

Affairs to the Secretary of the Interior for the Year 1889. Washington, D.C.: Government Printing Office, 1889. 359.

3. "About Grant Institute." *The Pipe of Peace.* Genoa, Nebraska. July 5, 1891. 1.

4. "Regarding the Indian School." *The Pipe of Peace.* Genoa, Nebraska. July 31, 1891.

5. Daddario, Wilma. "They Get Milk Practically Every Day: The Genoa Indian Industrial School, 1884–1934." *Nebraska History* 73 (1992): 8.

6. *Report of the Commissioner of Indian Affairs to the Secretary of the Interior for the Year 1895.* 378.

7. *Ibid.*

8. Daddario, Wilma. "They Get Milk Practically Every Day." 9.

9. *The Indian Helper.* December 13, 1895.

10. Letter from Chauncey Yellow Robe to William Pratt. June 9, 1897. Richard Henry Pratt Papers. Yale Collection of Western Americana, Beinecke Rare Book and Manuscript Library. Box 9, Folder 337.

11. Peavy, Linda S., and Ursula Smith. *Full-Court Quest: The Girls from Fort Shaw Indian School, Basketball Champions of the World.* Norman: University of Oklahoma Press, 2008. 390n, 399n.

12. *Sausalito* (California) *News* 11, no. 26 (August 3, 1895).

Chapter 10

1. *The Indian Helper.* October 29, 1897.

2. Segal, Jacqueline. *White Man's Club: Schools, Race, and the Struggle of Indian Acculturation.* Lincoln: University of Nebraska Press, 2007. 207.

3. Weinberg, Marjorie. *The Real Rosebud: The Triumph of a Lakota Woman.* Lincoln: University of Nebraska Press, 2004. 22.

4. *The Indian Helper.* August 26, 1898.

5. *The Indian Helper.* February 11, 1898.

6. *The Indian Helper.* May 5, 1899.

7. Weinberg, Marjorie. *The Real Rosebud.* 23.

8. *The Indian Helper.* July 6, 1899. Weinberg, Marjorie. *The Real Rosebud.* 23–24.

9. *Report of the Commissioner of Indian Affairs to the Secretary of the Interior for the Year 1899.* Washington, D.C.: Government Printing Office, 1899. 630.

10. *The Indian Helper.* July 6, 1899. Weinberg, Marjorie. *The Real Rosebud.* 23.

11. *Report of the Commissioner of Indian Affairs to the Secretary of the Interior for the Year 1900.* Washington, D.C.: Government Printing Office, 1900. 712.

12. *Report of the Commissioner of Indian Affairs to the Secretary of the Interior for the Year 1901.* Washington, D.C.: Government Printing Office, 1901. 735.

13. *Report of the Commissioner of Indian Affairs to the Secretary of the Interior for the Year 1902.* Washington, D.C.: Government Printing Office, 1902. 680.

14. Riney, Scott. *The Rapid City Indian School, 1898–1933.* Norman: University of Oklahoma Press, 1999. 167.

15. Letter from Jesse F. House, Superintendent of Rapid City Indian School to Commissioner of Indian Affairs. September 23, 1913. National Archives—Central Plains Office. Box 15. Code 161.

16. *Red Man and Helper.* December 25, 1903.

17. Record of Chauncey Yellow Robe. Form 5-351. National Archives—Central Plains Office. Box 15. Code 161.

Chapter 11

1. Riney, Scott. *The Rapid City Indian School, 1898–1933.* Norman: University of Oklahoma Press, 1999. 167.

2. Letter from Jesse F. House, Superintendent of Rapid City Indian School, to Commissioner of Indian Affairs. September 23, 1913. National Archives—Central Plains Office. Box 15. Code 161.

3. Mote, John A. *Growing Up with the American Indians.* Denver, Colorado: Outskirts, 2006. 30.

4. Memorandum from S.A.M. Young, Superintendent of Rapid City Indian School, to Chauncey Yellow Robe and Mrs. Walters. October 23, 1923. National Archives—Central Plains Office. Box 15. Code 161.

5. Riney, Scott. *The Rapid City Indian School.* 152.

6. Memorandum from Sharon Mote, Superintendent of Rapid City Indian School, to Mr. Fox, Rouillard, Basler. Cc to Chauncey Yellow Robe. December 15, 1925. National Archives—Central Plains Office. Box 15. Code 161.

7. Handwritten note from Sharon Mote, Superintendent of Rapid City Indian School, to Chauncey Yellow Robe. January 5, 1927. National Archives—Central Plains Office. Box 15. Code 161.

8. Memorandum from Sharon Mote, Superintendent of Rapid City Indian School, to Chauncey Yellow Robe and Mrs. Walters. February 2, 1926. National Archives—Central Plains Office. Box 15. Code 161.

9. Memorandum from Sharon Mote, Superintendent of Rapid City Indian School, to Chauncey Yellow Robe and (school matron). September 30 1927. National Archives—Central Plains Office. Box 15. Code 161.

10. Memorandum from Sharon Mote, Superintendent of Rapid City Indian School, to Chauncey Yellow Robe. June 29, 1927. National Archives—Central Plains Office. Box 15. Code 161.

11. Letter from James H. McGregor, District Superintendent, to Sharon R. Mote, Superintendent, Rapid City Indian School. January 26, 1928. National Archives—Central Plains Office. Box 15. Code 161.

12. Letter from Sharon R. Mote, Superintendent, Rapid City Indian School, to James H. McGregor, District Superintendent to School. February 20, 1928. National Archives—Central Plains Office. Box 15. Code 161.

13. Assistant Commissioner of Indian Affairs E.B. Merill to Sharon R. Mote, Superintendent, Rapid City Indian School. March 21, 1928. National Archives—Central Plains Office. Box 15. Code 161.

14. Letter from James H. McGregor, District Superintendent, to Sharon R. Mote, Superintendent, Rapid City Indian School. March 1, 1928. National Archives—Central Plains Office. Box 15. Code 161.

15. Notes in margins from Sharon R. Mote, Superintendent, Rapid City Indian School, to James H. McGregor, District Superintendent to School. March 9, 1928. National Archives—Central Plains Office. Box 15. Code 161.

16. Letter from Chauyncey Yellow Robe to J.F. House, Superintendent, Rapid City Indian School. September 8, 1917. National Archives—Central Plains Office. Box 15. Code 161

17. Riney, Scott. *The Rapid City Indian School.* 212.

18. Mote, John A. *Growing Up with the American Indians.* 30–31.

19. Sobel, Robert. *Coolidge: An American Enigma.* Washington, D.C.: Regnery, 2012. 368.

20. "Native History: Pres. Coolidge Summers in Black Hills, Adopted By Sioux." *Indian Country Today*, June 23, 2015. indiancountrymedianetwork.com. Accessed June 23, 2015.

21. O'Harra, C.C. "President Coolidge in the Black Hills." *Black Hills Engineer.* November 1927. Quoted by Weinberg, Marjorie. *The Real Rosebud: The Triumph of a Lakota Woman.* Lincoln: University of Nebraska Press, 2004. 35.

22. *Sioux County Pioneer.* June 23, 1927.

Chapter 12

1. "History of Spokane Deaconess Hospital." Program. Deaconess Hospital Alumni Reunion. June 1967.

2. Weinberg, Marjorie. *The Real Rosebud: The Triumph of a Lakota Woman.* Lincoln: University of Nebraska Press, 2004. 26.

3. *Ibid.*

4. *Ibid.*

5. Ellinghaus, Katherine. *Taking Assimilation to Heart: Marriages of White Women and Indigenous Men in the United States and Australia, 1887–1937.* Lincoln: University of Nebraska Press, 2006. xiii.

6. *Ibid.*, 55.

7. Weinberg, Marjorie. *The Real Rosebud.* 28.

8. Lily B. Y. Robe. Death Certificate. Number 109739. Filed May 10, 1927. South Dakota Board of Health.

9. Mote, John A. *Growing Up with the*

Chapter Notes—13 and 14

American Indians. Denver, Colorado: Outskirts, 2006. 30.

Chapter 13

1. Yellow Robe, Chauncey. "My Boyhood Days." *The American Indian Magazine* IV, no. 1 (1916): 50–53

2. Robe, Rosebud, and Jerry Pinkney. *Tonweya and the Eagles: And Other Lakota Indian Tales.* New York: Dial, 1979. 12.

3. Bear, Luther. *My People, the Sioux.* Lincoln: University of Nebraska Press, 1975. 10.

4. Alfred A. Frantz to Karen W. Moy. May 24, 1973. South Dakota Historical Society. H75.11/15. Also April 5, 1975.

5. Oneroad, Amos E., and Alanson B. Skinner. *Being Dakota: Tales and Traditions of the Sisseton and Wahpeton.* Edited by Laura L. Anderson. St. Paul: Minnesota Historical Society Press, 2003. 64.

6. Powers, William. *Oglala Religion.* Lincoln: University of Nebraska Press, 1977. 40.

7. Chauncey Yellow Robe to Doane Robinson. December 8, 1908. South Dakota Historical Society. Box 3359A, Folder 9.

8. Doane Robinson to Chauncey Yellow Robe. December 8, 1908. May 24, 1973. South Dakota Historical Society. Box 3359A, Folder 9.

9. "Sitting Bull Not Fighter but Agitator." *The Kokomo Tribune*, September 7, 1926.

10. Chief Clerk of the Library of Congress to Sharon Mote. October 19, 1928. National Archives—Central Plains Region. Kansas City, Missouri. Rapid City Indian School (75.RC). Box 15, Code 161.

11. Sharon Mote to Chauncey Yellow Robe. October 23, 1928. National Archives—Central Plains Region. Kansas City, Missouri. Rapid City Indian School (75.RC). Box 15, Code 161.

12. Sharon Mote to Commissioner of Indian Affairs. October 23, 1928. National Archives—Central Plains Region. Kansas City, Missouri. Rapid City Indian School (75.RC). Box 15, Code 161.

13. Alfred A. Frantz to Karen W. Moy. January 17, 1975. South Dakota Historical Society. H75.11/15.

Chapter 14

1. Robe, Rosebud, and Jerry Pinkney. *Tonweya and the Eagles: And Other Lakota Indian Tales.* New York: Dial, 1979. 16.

2. Weinberg, Marjorie. *The Real Rosebud: The Triumph of a Lakota Woman.* Lincoln: University of Nebraska Press, 2004. 30.

3. *The Papers of the Society of American Indians.* Edited by John W. Larner Jr. Wilmington, Del.: Scholarly Resources, 1987. Arthur Parker, S.A.I. Secretary-Treasurer to "Fellow Member." August 21, 1913. Michigan State University Library. 24346 Microfilm.

4. Chauncey Yellow Robe to Carlos Montezuma. May 6, 1912. The Papers of Carlos Montezuma, M.D., including the Papers of Maria Keller Montezuma Moore and the Papers of Joseph W. Latimer. Emory University. Woodruff Library Microfilm (MICFILM 1298).

5. Chauncey's brother, Joseph, was a member of the Buffalo Bill troop that toured Europe in 1906. His name is included with others in the troop who were passengers on the *Zeeland* both to Antwerp, Belgium, from New York and then back in 1906. Passenger and Immigration Lists Index, 1500s–1900s, record of Joseph Yellow Robe. Original data: Filby, P. William, ed. *Passenger and Immigration Lists Index, 1500s–1900s.* Farmington Hills, MI, USA: Gale Research.

6. Yellow Robe, Chauncey. "The Menace of the Wild West Show." *The Quarterly Journal of the Society of American Indians* II, no. 3 (1914): 224–25.

7. Chauncey Yellow Robe to Carlos Montezuma. December 22, 1913. The Papers of Carlos Montezuma, M.D., including the Papers of Maria Keller Montezuma Moore and the Papers of Joseph W. Latimer. Emory University. Woodruff Library Microfilm (MICFILM 1298).

8. Yellow Robe, Chauncey. "The Fighting Sioux." *The Quarterly Journal of the Society of American Indians* V, no. 4 (1917): 226–227.

9. "Editorial Views." *The Quarterly Journal of the Society of American Indians* V, no. 4 (1917): 217.

10. Denslow, William R. *Freemasonry and the American Indian*. St. Louis: Missouri Lodge of Research, 1956. iii.
11. Porter, Joy. *Native American Freemasonry: Associationalism and Performance in America*. Lincoln: University of Nebraska Press, 2011. 145.
12. Parker, Arthur C. "American Indians in Freemasonry." *The Builder* VIII, no. 3 (March 1922), also quoted in Denslow, William R. *Freemasonry and the American Indian*. St. Louis: Missouri Lodge of Research, 1956. 85.
13. Shunk, Harold. "One Indian's Story: Chauncey Yellow Robe." *Knight Templar*, January 1985, 5.

Chapter 15

1. Chauncey Yellow Robe to Carlos Montezuma. November 11, 1911. The Papers of Carlos Montezuma, M.D., including the Papers of Maria Keller Montezuma Moore and the Papers of Joseph W. Latimer. Emory University. Woodruff Library Microfilm (MICFILM 1298).
2. Ibid.
3. Chauncey Yellow Robe to Carlos Montezuma. December 8, 1913. The Papers of Carlos Montezuma, M.D., including the Papers of Maria Keller Montezuma Moore and the Papers of Joseph W. Latimer. Emory University. Woodruff Library Microfilm (MICFILM 1298).
4. Hertzsberg, Hazel W. *The Search for an American Indian Identity: Modern Pan-Indian Movements*. Syracuse, NY: Syracuse University Press, 1971. 119.
5. Chauncey Yellow Robe to Carlos Montezuma. March 27, 1913. The Papers of Carlos Montezuma, M.D., including the Papers of Maria Keller Montezuma Moore and the Papers of Joseph W. Latimer. Emory University. Woodruff Library Microfilm (MICFILM 1298).
6. Montezuma, Carlos. "Let My People Go." *The American Indian Magazine* published as *The Quarterly Journal of the Society of American Indians* IV, no. 1 (January–March 1916): 33.

Chapter 16

1. Gilbertson, Brian J. "The Native American Warriors in the U.S. Military." Master's Thesis, Unites States Marine Corp Conference Group 4, Command and Staff College, 2011. 19.
2. Britten, Thomas A. *American Indians in World War I: At Home and at War*. Albuquerque: University of New Mexico Press, 1997. 65.
3. *Report of the Commissioner of Indian Affairs to the Secretary of the Interior for the Year 1895*. Washington, D.C.: Government Printing Office, 1917. 6.
4. Letter from Chauncey Yellow Robe to William Pratt. Nov. 22, 1917. Richard Henry Pratt Papers. Yale Collection of Western Americana, Beinecke Rare Book and Manuscript Library. Box 9, Folder 337.
5. Britten, Thomas A. *American Indians in World War I*. 66.
6. Hoxie, Frederick E. *Talking Back to Civilization: Indian Voices from the Progressive Era*. Boston: Bedford/St. Martin's, 2001. 127.
7. Britten, Thomas A. *American Indians in World War I*. 64.
8. *Report of the Commissioner of Indian Affairs to the Secretary of the Interior for the Year 1918*. Washington, D.C.: Government Printing Office, 1918. 10.
9. Ibid., 9.
10. Britten, Thomas A. *American Indians in World War I*. 54.
11. Montezuma, Carlos, "Drafting Indians and Justice." *Wassaja* 2, no. 7 (October 1917): 3.
12. Britten, Thomas A. *American Indians in World War I*. 39.
13. Letter from Chauncey Yellow Robe to William Pratt. April 7, 1917. Richard Henry Pratt Papers. Yale Collection of Western Americana, Beinecke Rare Book and Manuscript Library. Box 9, Folder 337.
14. Letter from Chauncey Yellow Robe to William Pratt. April 15, 1917. Richard Henry Pratt Papers. Yale Collection of Western Americana, Beinecke Rare Book and Manuscript Library. Box 9, Folder 337.
15. *Report of the Commissioner of Indian*

Affairs to the Secretary of the Interior for the Year 1918. Washington, D.C.: Government Printing Office, 1918. 7.

16. Title of the section concerning the Great War in the report of Commissioner of Indian Affairs Cato Sells for 1919. September 30, 1919. In *The American Indian and the United States: A Documentary History*, vol. II. Ed. Wilcomb E. Washburn. New York: Random House, 1973, pp. 894–96.

17. Letter from Chauncey Yellow Robe to William Pratt. Nov. 11, 1917. Richard Henry Pratt Papers. Yale Collection of Western Americana, Beinecke Rare Book and Manuscript Library. Box 9, Folder 337.

18. Letter from Chauncey Yellow Robe to William Pratt. May 20, 1919. Richard Henry Pratt Papers. Yale Collection of Western Americana, Beinecke Rare Book and Manuscript Library. Box 9, Folder 337.

19. Britten, Thomas A. *American Indians in World War I*. 82

20. Letter from Chauncey Yellow Robe to William Pratt. April 25, 1917. Richard Henry Pratt Papers. Yale Collection of Western Americana, Beinecke Rare Book and Manuscript Library. Box 9, Folder 337.

21. Britten, Thomas A. *American Indians in World War I*. 81.

22. *Ibid.*, 160.

23. Letter from Chauncey Yellow Robe to William Pratt. November 30, 1918. Richard Henry Pratt Papers. Yale Collection of Western Americana, Beinecke Rare Book and Manuscript Library. Box 9, Folder 337.

24. Letter from Chauncey Yellow Robe to William Pratt. May 20, 1919. Richard Henry Pratt Papers. Yale Collection of Western Americana, Beinecke Rare Book and Manuscript Library. Box 9, Folder 337.

25. Britten, Thomas A. *American Indians in World War I*. 178.

26. *Ibid.*, 181

27. Letter from Chauncey Yellow Robe to William Pratt. June 21, 1917. Richard Henry Pratt Papers. Yale Collection of Western Americana, Beinecke Rare Book and Manuscript Library. Box 9, Folder 337.

28. Letter from Chauncey Yellow Robe to William Pratt. Nov. 22, 1917. Richard Henry Pratt Papers. Yale Collection of Western Americana, Beinecke Rare Book and Manuscript Library. Box 9, Folder 337.

Chapter 17

1. Letter from Chauncey Yellow Robe to William Pratt. January 14, 1919. Richard Henry Pratt Papers. Yale Collection of Western Americana, Beinecke Rare Book and Manuscript Library. Box 9, Folder 337

2. "The Influenza Epidemic of 1918." National Archives and Records Administration. Accessed August 3, 2015.

3. Letter from Jesse House, Superintendent to Mr. Kephart, farmer, Blackpipe District. October 4, 1918. National Archives—Central Plains Office. Box 106. Code 161.

4. Letter from Henry Tidwell, superintendent of the Pine Ridge Agency, to Jesse House. October 4, 1918. National Archives—Central Plains Office. Box 106. Code 161.

5. Letter from Jesse House to Henry Tidwell, superintendent of the Pine Ridge Agency, October 5, 1918. National Archives—Central Plains Office. Box 106. Code 161.

6. Letter from Jesse House to Henry Tidwell, superintendent of the Pine Ridge Agency, October 5, 1918. National Archives—Central Plains Office. Box 106. Code 161

7. Letter from Jesse House to Commissioner of Indian Affairs. October 5, 1918. National Archives—Central Plains Office. Box 106. Code 161

8. Letter from C.J. Crandall, superintendent at the Indian School in Pierre, to Jesse House. October 31, 1918. National Archives—Central Plains Office. Box 106. Code 161

9. Letter from Jesse House to Commissioner of Indian Affairs. October 12, 1918. National Archives—Central Plains Office. Box 106. Code 161.

10. Letter from Dr. L.L. Culp, Indian Commission special physician, to Commissioner of Indian Affairs. November 11, 1918. National Archives—Central Plains Office. Box 106. Code 161.

11. Letter from C.J. Crandall, superintendent at the Indian School in Pierre, to Jesse House. October 23, 1918. National Archives—Central Plains Office. Box 106. Code 161.

12. Letter from Dr. L.L. Culp, Indian Commission special physician, to House. November 6, 1918. National Archives—Central Plains Office. Box 106. Code 161.

13. Letter from Jesse House to Henry Tidwell, superintendent of the Pine Ridge Agency, October 28, 1918. National Archives—Central Plains Office. Box 106. Code 161.

14. Letter from Assistant Commissioner E.B. Merritt to Jesse House, December 11, 1918. National Archives—Central Plains Office. Box 106. Code 161.

15. Letter from Jesse House to (addressed to the Commissioner of Indian Affairs) responding to E.B. Merritt, assistant commissioner of Indian Affairs. December 16, 1918. National Archives—Central Plains Office. Box 106. Code 161.

16. Letter from Jesse House to Representative Harry Gandy. December 19, 1918. National Archives—Central Plains Office. Box 106. Code 161.

17. Letter from Jesse House to Commissioner of Indian Affairs. February 10, 1919. National Archives—Central Plains Office. Box 106. Code 161.

18. Letter from Jesse House to W.P. Marshall, farmer at Cherry Creek. November 18, 1918. National Archives—Central Plains Office. Box 106. Code 161

19. Riney, Scott. *The Rapid City Indian School, 1898–1933*. Norman: University of Oklahoma Press, 1999. 72.

Chapter 18

1. Yellow Robe, Chauncey. "The Menace of the Wild West Show." *The Quarterly Journal of the Society of American Indians* II, no. 3 (1914): 225.

2. *Rocky Mountain Daily News*, October 16, 1913. 7.

3. *Rapid City Daily Journal*, October 5, 1913. 5.

4. Miles, Nelson Appleton. *Serving the Republic: Memoirs of the Civil and Military Life of Nelson A. Miles, Lieutenant-General, United States Army*. New York: Harper & Bros., 1911. 243.

5. *The Denver Post*. March 9, 1914. 2.

6. The *Omaha Evening Bee*. November 4, 1913. 5.

7. *Rocky Mountain Daily News*, October 17, 1913. 3.

8. Letter from Claudia Kaulfuss, managing director of the Karl May Museum, to Cecil Pavlat, cultural repatriation specialist, Ojibwa Nation. March 12, 2014. Referenced with link in Melissa Eddy, "Lost in Translation: Germany's Fascination with the American Old West," *The New York Times*, August 18, 2014.

Chapter 19

1. *The Silent Enemy*. Performed by Chauncey Yellow Robe. Milestone Film & Video, 1992. Film. Original work: *The Silent Enemy*. United States: Paramount-Publix Corp., 1930. Film. Chauncey Yellow Robe speaking as Chief Yellow Robe.

2. Churchill, Ward. "American Indians in Film: Thematic Contours of Cinematic Colonization." In Xing, Jun, and Lane Ryo Hirabayashi, eds. *Reversing the Lens: Ethnicity, Race, Gender, and Sexuality through Film*. Boulder: University Press of Colorado, 2003. 43.

3. Schrom, Benjamin. "The Silent Enemy." 2008. http://www.silentfilm.org/archive/the-silent-enemy-1930. Accessed August 5, 2015.

4. 5. McBride, Bunny. *Molly Spotted Elk: A Penobscot in Paris*. Norman: University of Oklahoma Press, 1997. 100.

5. Reilly, Rosa. "Long Lance, Chief of Heart-Breakers." *Screenland*, October 1, 1930. 62–64. Chief Buffalo Long Lace Fond. Glenbow Museum. Calgary, BC.

6. Long, Sylvester. "Origins of Names among the Cherokees." *The Red Man* 3, no. 4. 173–175.

7. Smith, Donald B. *Chief Buffalo Child Long Lance: The Glorious Imposter*. Red Deer, Alberta: Red Deer Press, 1999. 76.

8. Smith, Donald B. *Chief Buffalo Child Long Lance*. 221, 252–254.

9. *Ibid.*, 226.
10. *Ibid.*, 266.
11. Smith, Donald B. *Chief Buffalo Child Long Lance.* 267.
12. McBride, Bunny. *Molly Spotted Elk: A Penobscot in Paris.* Norman: University of Oklahoma Press, 1997. 167
13. *Ibid.*, 286.
14. McBride, Bunny. *Molly Spotted Elk.*
15. "1920 All-Native Cast Silent Film 'The Daughter of Dawn' Premieres." Indian Country Today Media Network.com. http://indiancountrytodaymedianetwork.com/2013/04/23/1920-all-native-cast-silent-film-daughter-dawn-premieres-148980. Accessed August 5, 2015.
16. "The Daughter of Dawn." http://www.okhistory.org/research/daughterofdawn. Accessed August 5, 2015.

Chapter 20

1. Weinberg, Marjorie. *The Real Rosebud: The Triumph of a Lakota Woman.* Lincoln: University of Nebraska Press, 2004. 35.
2. Yellow Robe, Rosebud. Interview by Herbert Hoover. April 23, 1983. Transcript. University of South Dakota. Institute of American Indian Studies, South Dakota Oral History Center. Vermillion, South Dakota.
3. Yellow Robe, Rosebud. Interview by Herbert Hoover. April 23, 1983. Transcript. University of South Dakota. Institute of American Indian Studies, South Dakota Oral History Center. Vermillion, South Dakota.
4. Record of Marriage, Louis A. Roubideaux to Chaucina Yellow Robe, 23 May 1928, Fall River County, South Dakota. Number 124399. South Dakota State Board of Health, Pierre. (Note: The date of marriage on the Record of Divorce is 1929.)
5. Yellow Robe, Rosebud. Interview by Herbert Hoover. April 23, 1983. Transcript. University of South Dakota. Institute of American Indian Studies, South Dakota Oral History Center. Vermillion, South Dakota.
6. Record of Divorce, Louis A. Roubideaux from Chaucina Yellow Robe, 21 September 1932, Tripp County, South Dakota. Number 17593 South Dakota State Board of Health, Pierre, South Dakota. (note: The date of marriage on the Record of Marriage is 1928)
7. Yellow Robe, Rosebud. Interview by Herbert Hoover. April 23, 1983. Transcript. University of South Dakota. Institute of American Indian Studies, South Dakota Oral History Center. Vermillion, South Dakota.
8. *Ibid.*
9. Weinberg, Marjorie. *The Real Rosebud: The Triumph of a Lakota Woman.* Lincoln: University of Nebraska Press, 2004. 58–29.
10. Fielder, Mildred. *Sioux Indian Leaders.* New York: Bonanza, 1981. 125–126.
11. Letter from Rosebud Yellow Robe to Mildred Fielder. March 26, 1976. Mildred Fielder Collection. Devereaux Library. South Dakota School of Mines and Technology. Rapid City, SD.
12. Dockstader, Frederick J. *Great North American Indians: Profiles in Life and Leadership.* New York: Van Nostrand Reinhold, 1977. 346.
13. "Carlisle Indian to Run for Congress." *Carlisle Indian*, December 12, 1927. Reprinted from *The Evening Sentinel, Monday, December 12, 192.*
14. Letter from Chauncey Yellow Robe to Editor, *Hot Springs Star.* August 24, 1928. Rosebud Yellow Robe Franz Collection. H75.11/16. South Dakota State Historical Research Center. Pierre, SD.
15. Letter from Chauncey Yellow Robe to Commissioner of Indian Affairs (through Superintendent Mote). August 8, 1928. National Archives—Central Plains Office. Box 106. Code 161

Chapter 21

1. Weinberg, Marjorie. *The Real Rosebud: The Triumph of a Lakota Woman.* Lincoln: University of Nebraska Press, 2004. xvi.
2. Letter from Della Vik to Mildred Fielder. May 17, 1969. Mildred Fielder

Collection. Devereaux Library. South Dakota School of Mines and Technology. Rapid City, SD.

3. Yellow Robe, Rosebud. Interview by Herbert Hoover. April 23, 1983. Transcript. University of South Dakota. Institute of American Indian Studies, South Dakota Oral History Center. Vermillion, South Dakota.

4. Schultz, Rima Lunin, and Adele Hast, eds. *Chicago 1790–1990: A Biographical Dictionary*. Bloomington: Indiana University Press, 2001. 962–964.

5. Yellow Robe, Rosebud. Interview by Herbert Hoover. April 23, 1983. Transcript. University of South Dakota. Institute of American Indian Studies, South Dakota Oral History Center. Vermillion, South Dakota.

6. *Ibid.*
7. *Ibid.*
8. *Ibid.*

9. White Horse, Chaucina. "The Indians of Chicago: A Perspective." Typed Manuscript. N.A.E.S. College Library. 86.

10. . Letter from Rosebud Yellow Robe to Mildred Fielder. March 26, 1976. Mildred Fielder Collection. Devereaux Library. South Dakota School of Mines and Technology. Rapid City, SD

11. Letter from Della Vik to Mildred Fielder. May 17, 1969. Mildred Fielder Collection. Devereaux Library. South Dakota School of Mines and Technology. Rapid City, SD.

12. "Evelyn Yellowrobe, New in Speech Dept. Descendant of Famous Sitting Bull." *The Mount Holyoke News*, February 18, 1944.

13. "Wins Indian Medal." September 23, 1946. Mount Holyoke College Archives, South Hadley, MA.

14. "Miss Yellow Robe Named to Film Group." *New Yorker*, December 30, 1949. Clipping on file at the Mount Holyoke College Archives, South Hadley, MA.

15. "Song in Honor of Tasingai." Charles Red Breath Bear. Evelyn Robe Finkbeiner Collection of Dakota Songs. American Folklife Center, Washington, D.C.

Chapter 22

1. Masonic Code of South Dakota Constitution and By-Laws of the Grand Lodge of Ancient, Free and Accepted Masons of South Dakota. Revised and ordered printed by The Grand Lodge 201375.75.

2. "Chief Yellow Robe, Sioux Educator Dies; Devoted Most of His 63 Years to His People." *New York Times*, April 8, 1930, Obituary sec.

3. Email from Marjorie Weinberg to Cumberland County Historical Society. April, 2000.

4. "Yellow Robe to be Buried Sunday." *The Rapid City Journal*, April 10, 1930. Obituary sec.

5. Robe, Rosebud, and Jerry Pinkney. *Tonweya and the Eagles: And Other Lakota Indian Tales*. New York: Dial, 1979. 17–18.

Chapter 23

The information and opinions in this chapter were expressed by members of the extended Yellow Robe family in a series of conversations and emails with the author.

Chapter 24

1. Yellow Robe, Chauncey. "My Boyhood Days." *The American Indian Magazine* IV, no. 1 (1916): 50–53.

2. Lookingbill, Brad D. *War Dance at Fort Marion: Plains Indian War Prisoners*. Norman: University of Oklahoma Press, 2006. 115.

3. Weinberg, Marjorie. *The Real Rosebud the Triumph of a Lakota Woman*. Lincoln: University of Nebraska Press, 2004. 21.

Bibliography

Books and Articles

Adams, David Wallace. *Education for Extinction: American Indians and the Boarding School Experience, 1875–1928.* Lawrence: University of Kansas, 1995.

Archuleta, Margaret L., Brenda J. Child, and K. Tsianina Lomawaima, eds. *Away from Home: American Indian Boarding School Experiences, 1879–2000.* Phoenix, AZ: Heard Museum, 2000.

Biolsi, Thomas. *Deadliest Enemies: Law and Race Relations On and Off Rosebud Reservation.* Minneapolis: University of Minnesota, 2007.

Blaisdell, Robert. *Great Speeches by Native Americans.* Mineola, NY: Dover, 2000.

Britten, Thomas A. *American Indians in World War I.* Albuquerque: University of New Mexico Press, 1997.

Buffalo Bill. *Buffalo Bill's Life Story: An Autobiography.* New York: Skyhorse, 2010.

"Buffalo Bill's Wild West Indians." *Washington Post,* August 5, 1890.

"Chauney Yellow Robe Follow-Up." *Knight Templar,* February 1986, 15.

"Chief Yellow Robe, Sioux Educator Dies; Devoted Most of His 63 Years to His People." *New York Times,* April 8, 1930.

Coleman, Michael C. *American Indian Children at School, 1850–1930.* Jackson: University of Mississippi, 2008.

Daddario, Wilma. "They Get Milk Practically Every Day: The Genoa Indian Industrial School, 1884–1934." *Nebraska History* 73 (1992): 8.

"Dakota Images: Chauncey Yellow Robe." *South Dakota History* (Spring 1979).

"Dakota Images: Chauncey Yellow Robe." *South Dakota History* (Spring 1992).

Debo, Angie. *A History of the Indians of the United States.* Norman: University of Oklahoma, 1970.

Deloria, Vine. *God Is Red: A Native View of Religion.* Golden, CO: Fulcrum, 2003.

Dockstader, Frederick J. *Great North American Indians: Profiles in Life and Leadership.* New York: Van Nostrand Reinhold, 1977.

"Don't Agree with Them." *Wheeling Register,* June 16, 1890.

Ellinghaus, Katherine. *Taking Assimilation to Heart: Marriages of White Women and Indigenous Men in the United States and Australia, 1887–1937.* Lincoln: University of Nebraska, 2006.

Erdoes, Richard, and Alphonso Ortiz. *Native American Myths and Legends.* New York: Pantheon, 1984.

Fear-Segal, Jacqueline. *White Man's Club: Schools, Race, and the Struggle of Indian Acculturation.* Lincoln: University of Nebraska, 2007.

Bibliography

Feest, Christian F., ed. *Indians and Europe: An Interdisciplinary Collection of Essays*. Lincoln: University of Nebraska, 1999.
Fielder, Mildred. *Sioux Indian Leaders*. New York: Bonanza, 1975.
Fielder, Mildred. "War Whoop!" *Rapid City Journal* (May 11, 1969): 24.
Fire, John, and Richard Erdoes. *Lame Deer, Seeker of Visions*. New York: Simon & Schuster, 1972.
Flood, Reneé S. *Lost Bird of Wounded Knee: Spirit of the Lakota*. New York: Scribner's, 1995.
Gibbon, Guy E. *The Sioux: The Dakota and Lakota Nations*. Malden, MA: Blackwell, 2003.
Gridley, Marion E. *Indians of Today*. Chicago, 1936.
Heise, Kenan. "Native American Writer Robert White Horse." *Chicago Tribune*, October 25, 1997.
Hertzberg, Hazel W. *The Search for an American Indian Identity: Modern Pan-Indian Movements*. Syracuse, NY: Syracuse University Press, 1981.
Hoxie, Frederick E. *A Final Promise: The Campaign to Assimilate the Indians, 1880–1920*. Lincoln: University of Nebraska, 1984.
Hoxie, Frederick E. *Talking Back to Civilization: Indian Voices from the Progressive Era*. Boston: Bedford/St. Martins, 2001.
Larson, Erik. *The Devil in the White City: Murder, Magic and Madness at the Fair That Changed America*. New York: Vintage, 2004.
Liberty, Margot. *American Indian Intellectuals of the Nineteenth and Early Twentieth Centuries*. Norman: University of Oklahoma, 2002.
Lomawaima, K. Tsianina. *They Called It Prairie Light: The Story of Chilocco Indian School*. Lincoln: University of Nebraska, 1994.
Luschei, Martin. *The Black Hills and the Indians: A Haven of Our Hopes*. San Luis Obispo, CA: Niobrara, 2007.
Marshall, Joseph M. *The Journey of Crazy Horse: A Lakota History*. New York: Viking, 2004.
Marshall, Joseph. *To You We Shall Return: Lessons About Our Planet from the Lakota*. New York: Sterling Ethos, 2010.
McBride, Bunny. *Molly Spotted Elk: A Penobscot in Paris*. Norman and London: University of Oklahoma, 1995.
McGregor, James H. *The Wounded Knee Massacre: From the Viewpoint of the Sioux*. Rapid City, SD: Fenwyn, 1987.
McNeill, William Hardy. *Plagues and Peoples*. Garden City, NY: Anchor, 1976.
McNenly, Linda Scarangella. *Native Performers in Wild West Shows: From Buffalo Bill to Euro Disney*. Norman: University of Oklahoma, 2012.
Moses, L. G. *Wild West Shows and the Images of American Indians, 1883–1933*. Albuquerque: University of New Mexico, 1999.
Oneroad, Amos E. and Alanson B. Skinner. *Being Dakota: Tales and Traditions of the Sisseton and Wahpeton*. Edited by Laura L. Anderson. St. Paul: Minnesota Historical Society, 2003.
"Painted Horse." *Aberdeen Daily News*, November 11, 1890.
Paul, Andrea I. "Buffalo Bill and Wounded Knee: The Movie." *Nebraska History* (Winter 1990); 183–190.
Peavy, Linda S., and Ursula Smith. *Full-Court Quest: The Girls from Fort Shaw Indian School, Basketball Champions of the World*. Norman: University of Oklahoma, 2008.

Bibliography

Perdue, Theda. *Race and the Atlanta Cotton States Exposition of 1895*. Athens: University of Georgia, 2010.

Porter, Joy. *Native American Freemasonry: Associationalism and Performance in America*. Lincoln: University of Nebraska, 2011.

Pratt, Richard Henry. *Battlefield and Classroom: Four Decades with the American Indian, 1867–1904*. Edited by Robert M. Utley. Norman: University of Oklahoma, 2003.

Prucha, Francis Paul. *The Great Father: The United States Government and the American Indians*. Lincoln: University of Nebraska Press, 1986.

Richardson, Heather Cox. *Wounded Knee: Party Politics and the Road to an American Massacre*. New York: Basic, 2010.

Ricker, Eli Seavey. *Voices of the American West, Volume 1: The Indian Interviews of Eli S. Ricker, 1903–1919*. Edited by Richard E. Jensen. Lincoln: University of Nebraska, 2005.

Riney, Scott. *The Rapid City Indian School, 1898–1933*. Norman: University of Oklahoma, 1999.

Schultz, Rima Lunin, and Adele Hast, eds. *Women Building Chicago, 1790–1990: A Biographical Dictionary*. Bloomington: Indiana University Press, 2001.

Shunk, Harold W. "One Indian's Story: Chauncey Yellow Robe." *Knight Templar*, January 1985.

Smith, Donald B. *Long Lance: The Fascinating Life of an Imposter*. Red Deer, Alberta: Red Deer, 1999.

Sprague, Donovin Arleigh. *Rosebud Sioux*. Charleston, SC: Arcadia, 2005.

Standing Bear, Luther. *Land of the Spotted Eagle*. Lincoln: University of Nebraska, 1978.

Trafzer, Clifford E., Jean A. Keller, and Lorene Sisquoc, eds. *Boarding School Blues: Revisiting American Indian Educational Experiences*. Lincoln: University of Nebraska, 2006.

Walker, J. R. *The Sun Dance and Other Ceremonies of the Oglala Division of the Teton Dakota*. New York, 1917.

Warren, Louis S. *Buffalo Bill's America: William Cody and the Wild West Show*. New York: Alfred A. Knopf, 2005.

Weinberg, Marjorie. *The Real Rosebud: The Triumph of a Lakota Woman*. Lincoln: University of Nebraska, 2004.

Wilson, Jerry. "Remembering Genoa's Indian School." *Nebraska Life* (March/April 2008): 16–22.

Yellow Robe, Chauncey. Letter to the Editor, *Hot Springs Star*, August 24, 1928.

Yellow Robe, Chauncey. "My Boyhood Days." *The American Indian Magazine* IV, no. 1 (1916): 50–53.

Yellow Robe, Chauncey. "The World's Fair Seen by an Aborigine." *The Red Man*, February 1, 1895.

Yellow Robe, Rosebud, and Jerry Pinkney. *Tonweya and the Eagles: And Other Lakota Indian Tales*. New York: Dial for Young Readers, 1979.

Zitkala-Ša, with an Introduction by Susan Dominguez Rose. *American Indian Stories*. Lincoln: University of Nebraska, 2003.

Newspapers and Periodicals

The Indian Helper. 1887–1889.
The Red Man and Indian Helper. December 25, 1903.

Bibliography

Interviews

Finkbeiner, Evelyn. Daughter of Chauncey Yellow Robe. 2012.
Magnusson, Stew. Author of *The Death of Raymond Yellow Thunder* and *Wounded Knee: Still Bleeding*. 2012.
Maynard, Clair, Jr. Son of Clair F. Maynard, who was quoted in *Sioux Indian Leaders* by Mildred Fielder. 2011.
Nelson, Theresa. Granddaughter of William Yellow Robe, a brother of Chauncey Yellow Robe. 2012–2017.
Romero, Patty. Granddaughter of Joe Yellow Robe, a brother of Chauncey Yellow Robe. 2010–2017.
Staugler, Matt. Research assistant, Bicycle Museum of America. September 3, 2013.
Stitman, Fawn. Daughter of Chaucina Yellow Robe. July 12, 2012.
Weinberg, Marjorie. Author of *The Real Rosebud: The Triumph of a Lakota Woman*. 2010.
Yellow Robe, Luke. Great-grandson of Isaac Yellow Robe, a brother of Chauncey Yellow Robe. 2010.

Archives and Records

American Folklife Center, Washington, D.C.
Carlisle Indian School Research Collection, Cumberland County Historical Society, Carlisle, PA.
Deaconess Medical Center, Spokane, WA.
Denver Library and Archives, Denver Museum of Nature and Science.
Devereaux Library, South Dakota School of Mines and Technology.
Dickinson College Archives, Carlisle, PA.
Glenbow Museum, Calgary, Alberta.
Library of Congress.
Mount Holyoke College Archives and Special Collections.
National Archives, Kansas City. Records from Rapid City Indian School.
National Archives, Washington, D.C. Carlisle Indian School (Group 75, File 1327).
Papers of Carlos Montezuma.
Rapid City Library.
Richard Henry Pratt Papers, Beinecke Rare Book and Manuscript Library, Yale University.
Sinte Gleska University, Rosebud Sioux Reservation, Mission, SD.
Smithsonian Institution Museum Support Center, Washington, D.C.
South Dakota Oral History Center, Vermillion.
South Dakota State Historical Center, Office of Vital Statistics, Pierre.
South Dakota State Historical Society.
University of Wisconsin Library. Annual Reports of the Commissioner of Indian Affairs.
U.S. Indian Census Rolls, 1885–1940.
U.S. Social Security Death Index.
Yellow Robe family cemetery and former residences, Rosebud Sioux Reservation, Mission, SD.

Index

alcohol 15, 70, 113, 148
assimilation 2, 10, 18, 44, 48–49, 56. 74, 82, 87, 89, 95, 96, 98, 138, 152

Brule 14
Buffalo Child Long Lance 97. 98, 119–127

Carlisle Indian School 2, 5, 8, 9, 17–19, 22, 23, 25–27, 33–38, 41, 42, 44–46, 48, 49, 54–58, 60–62, 64, 65, 70, 82, 83, 86–88, 92, 97, 107, 120–123, 131, 133, 137, 138, 143, 144, 151, 152, 156, 157, 164, 170
Chicago American Indian Oral History Project 136
Chief Spotted Tail 17, 18, 36
Clark, Badger 10, 11, 155
Cody, Buffalo Bill 9, 39, 40, 45, 50, 53, 83, 97, 110–112, 117, 122, 145, 156, 160, 163, 164, 167–169; see also Wild West Show
Columbian Quadricentennial 9, 42
Coolidge, Calvin 70–72, 87, 131, 134, 143, 144, 159
Cotton States Exposition 50, 52, 53
creation story (Lakota) 13

Eastman, Charles 46, 74, 81–85, 87
education 17, 18, 25, 33, 34, 35, 42, 46, 49, 55, 82, 85, 92, 137, 138, 143, 151

Fort Lewis 60, 61, 64
Fort Marion 16, 17, 34, 151
Fort Shaw 58–62

haircut order 27
House, Jesse 73

interracial marriages 74, 75

Jordan, Charles Philander 50

Lakota 2, 7, 13–16, 30–32, 37, 65, 70, 71, 81, 107, 113, 129, 133, 135, 148, 155–160, 164, 165
Long, Sylvester 97, 123; see also Buffalo Child Long Lance

Masons 84, 85, 86, 141, 161, 170
Mather, Sarah 16, 17, 151, 152, 155
May, Karl 113, 114
Maynard, Claire 130, 131
Miles, Nelson 110, 112
Montezuma, Carols 2, 10, 46, 47, 74, 81–89, 95, 160, 161, 170
Mote, Sharon 65–69, 75, 76, 79, 132, 158–160, 164

naming 28, 29, 31, 32
Nelson, Molly 119, 124; see also Molly Spotted Elk

outing 34, 35, 38, 57, 61, 121: see also Carlisle Indian School

pan–Indianism 10, 49, 81
Pratt, Richard 2, 10, 16–19, 22–25, 33–36. 38, 39, 43–45, 47–49, 58, 61, 62, 64, 74, 82, 83, 86, 87, 95–97, 100, 101, 122, 123, 137, 151, 155–158, 161, 162, 169, 170

Rapid City Indian School 62, 65, 66, 73, 74, 91, 92, 100, 101, 106, 132, 134
Robinson, Doane 78, 160

171

Index

Sickles, Emma 43, 44
The Silent Enemy 19, 79, 115, 117, 119, 122, 123, 124, 138
Sitting Bull 19, 51, 52, 53, 77–80, 117, 119, 117, 119, 138, 144, 147
Society of American Indians 8, 49, 74, 81, 82, 85–889, 93, 95, 100, 110
Spanish flu 101–103, 105–107
Spotted Elk, Molly 119, 124, 126

Tasinagi 30
Thorpe, Jim 121, 122

Weinberg, Marjorie 7, 53, 54, 60, 61, 62, 74, 75, 81, 129, 130, 133, 134, 143, 146, 147
White House Conference on Aging 136
Whitehorse, Lee 136
Wild West Show 9, 10, 39, 44, 45, 53, 80, 82, 83, 97, 108, 111, 121; *see also* Buffalo Bill Cody
World War I 84, 89, 91, 93, 98, 100, 113
Wounded Knee 3, 14, 44, 80, 108–113, 117, 126, 149

Yellow Robe, Chaucina 75, 129–131, 133–136, 143, 145, 170
Yellow Robe, Evelyn 24, 75, 76, 129–131, 133 135, 137–140, 145, 165, 170
Yellow Robe (Springer), Lillian 63, 65, 73–78, 101, 144, 145, 150
Yellow Robe, Richard 24, 26, 30, 36
Yellow Robe, Rosebud 5–7, 14–17, 19, 22, 37, 38, 41, 42, 45, 49, 50, 52, 53, 61, 62, 64, 70–72, 75, 77–79, 81, 83, 129–131, 133–139, 143–148, 150, 153, 155–160, 164, 165, 167, 169, 170

www.ingramcontent.com/pod-product-compliance
Ingram Content Group UK Ltd.
Pitfield, Milton Keynes, MK11 3LW, UK
UKHW042016140426
5217IPUK00015B/1200